Your
Mom Walk
with God

Your Mom Walk with God

with God

Staying Faithful on the Path of Motherhood

Sally Clarkson

Whole Heart Press
Monument, CO

YOUR MOM WALK WITH GOD

Published by Whole Heart Press
A division of Whole Heart Ministries
PO Box 3445, Monument, CO 80132
www.wholeheart.org

ISBN: 978-1-888692-31-0

Previously published as
The Mom Walk

Third Edition
August 2016

Cover design by Flavius Petrisor
Interior design by Clay Clarkson
Illustration by Jennifer Trafton Peterson

Unless otherwise indicated, all Scripture verses are taken from the New American Standard Bible,® @ 1960, 1962, 1963, 1968, 1971, 1972, 1973, 1975, 1977, 1995 by The Lockman Foundation. Used by permission. (www.Lockman.org)

Printed in the United States of America

To my faithful and true
best friend and husband, Clay,
who has so patiently
walked the path of parenting
with me side by side.

Acknowledgments

I want to thank the Lord, as always, for so gently and patiently taking me through my journey of motherhood. Thank You for being my loving and encouraging companion.

Grateful thanks are also due ...

To Sarah, my sweet oldest daughter and friend, for helping to edit my writing of this book. You are so talented and skillful at making my hurried thoughts appear coherent. Thank you, Sarah, for reading my mind and always being available.

To Joel, Nathan, and Joy for also blessing me and being so understanding and supportive of our family's ministry lifestyle!

To Clay, for coming up with the PATH acrostic that provided an outline and metaphor for all the thoughts and stories I wanted to share.

To our diligent board members and all the precious families who invest time and personal resources in helping us reach more families all over the world. You make this ministry a pleasure for us to lead, and you make it possible for us to keep going. This book is because of your faithfulness in our lives. God bless you.

Contents

Walk with Me

Thus says the LORD, "Stand by the ways and
see and ask for the ancient paths, where the
good way is, and walk in it; and you will
find rest for your souls."

JEREMIAH 6:16

The rugged beauty of the Rocky Mountains fairly beckoned us to come outside to celebrate each morning as we awakened and prepared our coffee to savor on our deck. We had recently moved into a home situated at seventy-five hundred feet in the foothills at the western edge of Monument, Colorado. Pike's Peak was just down the ridge, and our extended backyard was twenty-five thousand acres of national forest. We were only just beginning to discover the wonderful trails and vistas that were open to us literally just walking out our back door.

One day as we were out for a walk through our neighborhood, a casual acquaintance riding a mountain bike near our home stopped to talk with us about his recent ride in the mountains.

"There is a spectacular vista from the mountain just above your house where you can see hundreds of miles in all directions. I think it's at nine thousand feet—about a fifteen hundred foot climb for you. It would probably take you only an hour or so to make the hike, and I think you and your kids would absolutely love the experience." He quickly told me how to get to the trailhead and wished me well before riding away.

I had been waiting for the right day, and today the calendar was free, the weather inviting, the air cool and crisp, and the sun shining. I announced to my four children—Sarah, 15; Joel, 12; Nathan, 10; and Joy, 4—that we would be going on a day hike and picnic in the high mountain area behind our house. I finished my preparations, packing a light lunch with egg salad finger sandwiches, bottles of water, grapes, and a couple of chocolate chip cookies for each of us. I wanted to keep the pack light because I knew I would have to carry Joy on my back part of the way.

After smearing sunscreen on everyone, finding Nathan's tennis shoes, and zipping up a light jacket on Joy, we opened the back door and began our adventure. Penny, our loyal golden retriever, trotted along behind us. I yelled goodbye to Clay, my husband, who was working on a deadline for our ministry. "We might be up there for several hours because I hear it is a great place to play," I said to him as I closed the back door.

I have to admit, I was feeling a little proud of being such a great mom—making an unforgettable memory, providing an adventure for my children, and supplying all we would need for our trip.

We found the trailhead within ten minutes and began the steep climb to the lookout. Sarah yelled a challenge to the boys, "Hey, let's run up the mountain and see who's first to the top!" The three older kids energetically took out at a run while I held Joy's hand and started a slower ascent. After about twenty minutes, we caught up with the more energetic group who were, by then, all sitting on the side of the pathway out of breath and panting from the thin mountain air.

"How much farther to the top?" questioned one of my boys. "I'm already tired and hungry!"

"Don't worry! My friend said we could probably make the whole hike in one hour, so in another fifteen minutes we should reach the top of the hill where there is a vista, and we will picnic there," I confidently assured him.

About twenty minutes later, panting and sweating, we all pulled up to a lovely vista that we *supposed* was the top of the mountain. I was so relieved because carrying Joy the last fifteen minutes had been quite taxing. Surely I had just finished the most arduous climb.

We discovered a lovely meadow a little bit beyond the cliff where we had been looking out over the valley and city below. Running through the grassy field, we discovered a tiny wood cabin that was weather-worn and half blown down. Sitting on the old logs and pulling out our lunch pleased us all. Amid the giggles and chattering, we decided to pretend that we were pioneers on the Oregon Trail. The kids ran around whooping and amusing themselves while I enjoyed the beauty and rested under the shade of an old pine. One of my children even found a small cross in the middle of a circle of stones that looked like an old gravesite. What an adventure as we imagined the story of the lives of people who had built a home so high in the mountains, who must have known deep joys and sorrows.

Feeling well-pleased with myself at the sweet memories we were making, we gathered around and thanked the Lord for our adventure and for giving us such a beautiful day. After packing up the litter from our picnic, we decided we were rested enough to complete the remainder of the hike to the end of the trail. Off we went on our journey with a renewed sense of adventure.

Within ten minutes, our path led to gigantic boulders and a small stream that led southward along the back of the mountain we had just climbed. The older three fearlessly began to climb the rocks that were twelve to twenty feet in height.

"Be careful! If you fall, I would have a hard time helping you because Joy and I can't climb up there." A tiny sense of irritation began to bubble up in my heart, which often surprises me in taxing moments of caring for my children's needs.

Why do they always have to run ahead? When will they offer to help with the pack? I shouldn't have to carry Joy and the pack all by myself! I didn't know how heavy Joy would be. I wish she could walk a little more on her own! Oh well, they are having fun. I should be mature and not allow myself to become irritated. It was my idea, after all.

I quickly tried to suppress these feelings because I didn't want anything to darken the anticipation of the wonderful adventure we had planned for this day. I recognized that my emotions were beginning to go a bit sour from being fatigued.

Making progress on the trail among the rocks was a bit slow. After about an hour, the kids rejoined Joy and me and asked for a drink. Each water bottle had just an inch of water left, but since we were certainly close to the end of the trail, I let everyone drink their last sip.

Why have we been hiking well over two hours and not come to the end of the trail? It must be because of the slower pace we are walking and from having young children with me. After all, my friend had been on a mountain bike. I can't imagine how he could have ridden his bike on these rough trails. Some people are just tougher than others.

The beauty and views of seemingly untouched wilderness awed and amazed us as we quietly walked forward on a now scarcely visible path. We wondered if it was a pathway made by deer leading to the stream. Picnicking and hiking need to become a regular activity, we unanimously agreed. "Aren't we happy we all moved to Colorado?" Sarah asked.

Gingerly we continued to walk forward along the faint trail, which by now had left the stream and led into the dark shadows of an overgrown pine forest. The path moved into the shadows along a very narrow trail on the side of the mountain. I began to perceive that everyone was becoming exhausted. The food was gone and it was time for Joy's nap. What had been a playful, rousing adventure at the start, when everyone was excited and filled with wonder, was slowly dissipating into a silent march as each of us focused on putting one foot in front of the other.

After a quiet fifteen minutes, Joel verbalized what we had all secretly been thinking. "Are we on the right trail? I thought we were supposed to be home by now. What if we are lost? Maybe we should go back. We might be in danger if we don't start back home soon."

Reflecting on the difficult time I had already had bringing Joy through the rough wall of rocks, I couldn't even imagine taking her back the same way without even greater effort. At least this trail was straight and not on a steep ascent, as the previous trail had been. Though I didn't know where it led, I was unwilling to go back on the more difficult part. We seemed to be heading toward the other end of our mountain. Surely we would come to the turning point soon.

"I think we will be okay, Joel, if we just keep going. It would take us almost two and a half hours to backtrack, and I am sure we will find the end of this trail soon. It probably leads around to the other part of the road, which leads right to our house. I think you kids have done amazingly well. What troopers you are and such amazing hikers! Daddy will be so proud of you when he finds out how well you have done."

I hoped my enthusiastic voice would not betray my hidden feelings of fear, exhaustion, and irritation at myself for not getting a map of the mountain. I had never really been on a primitive trail like this and was only beginning to realize how unprepared I had been for such a trek. I had heard of the "wildness" of the wilderness. It seemed that we were indeed in wilderness, as we had not passed another human being in our path for the last three hours. We pressed on.

ణ

Four hours later found us a pitiful, dirty, exhausted, and emotionally worn group of wanderers. We had walked hours in different terrains: through a forest, over rough rocks, passing a deep cave, foraging through brush, and walking on a dry, dusty path that covered us with reddish sand. Thinking of myself as a resourceful woman, I had pulled out my trusty cell phone several times and attempted to call Clay for help. How was I to know there wasn't cell reception in this part of the Rockies?

We had passed through multiple stages of kids whining and complaining, of sore feet, a series of "I can't go any further" tears, and fears of "What if we die on this mountain and get eaten up by a bear?" Accompanying this were accusations: "Why didn't you bring more water, Mom? Why didn't you find out exactly where we were supposed to go? Why did you bring us this far? How do you know we are going in the right direction? When are we ever going to make it home?"

My great mom-plans were turning into a series of bad, unprepared mom-moments of failure. The kids had indeed amazed me at their ability to persevere. Our faithful dog, Penny, had kept by our side. I felt as though we were living out a script of a Disney movie adventure about a family stranded in the wilds of a mountain looking for ways to survive.

Sarah and Joel had each carried forty-pound Joy on their backs for half-an-hour at a time, trying to give my aching back a break. I had been carrying her most of the afternoon as she became a dead-weight while napping in my arms or on my back. Every muscle in my body ached from carrying her half-stooped for a good deal of the time so that she wouldn't fall off my back in her sleep.

Nathan had pushed beyond his own penchant for complaining and had kept his strong young legs going far beyond my expectations. He even had bursts of energy from time to time as we came across an interesting scene. At one point we happened upon the wreck of an old car that looked as though it had driven off a cliff.

Joel had pushed beyond his fear about all the dangers and had decided to be the brave man of the group, encouraging us onward, telling us that the only choice we had was to keep going—as though he were trying to convince himself by saying it out loud.

I had moved through all sorts of stages of emotions: irritation, fear, tears, panic, courage, determination, and condemnation. My weary brain took on a burden of guilt. *How could I have led my children into this mess?*

We had stopped and prayed several times together, but I had been praying silently all along the way out of a growing desperation. *Please, God, lead us and get us out of this mess!*

The sun was setting as we finally found an old road that seemed to lead down the mountain toward the city lights below. I decided to try to call Clay again. The call actually got through this time. Bypassing his usual casual "Hello," I could hear the anxiety in his voice as he answered with a tense "Where are you?" I was so relieved to hear him, and I just quickly answered, "I don't know exactly, but we just need someone to pick us up..." at which point the phone went dead.

What I didn't know is that Clay had gone to get in the car, hoping he could drive on a back road to try to find us, only to discover the key would not work. It was a friend's car, since ours was in the shop, but the only key Clay could find for it wouldn't unlock the door, and the friends were not home. We found out later that one of the kids had put the good keys in a side pocket in my pack, somehow thinking we might need them! So Clay was stranded without transportation and unable to communicate with us, so he was left waiting for another call and wondering what in the world was happening to his family.

The children began to shiver in the evening mountain air and their teeth began to chatter. Of course, by this time we had been hours without food or water. All of us felt exceedingly thirsty and hungry. We stopped on the side of the road for a small rest and noticed the Air Force Academy sitting below us in the near distance. This let me know that we were quite high on the abandoned, almost impassable road. Just when I thought things couldn't get worse, a pack of coyotes nearby started howling at the moon.

"Mom, do coyotes attack people and eat them?" one of the boys fearfully questioned.

The other, more informed child answered, "They just attack small animals like Penny and Joy. They are the only ones in danger of being eaten!" Again, panic and chills of fear ran through us all as we walked in darkness, listening to the howling beasts.

At this moment, an angel, in the form of a motorcyclist in a black leather jacket, came along beside us and stopped. He pulled up his helmet so we could see his dark eyes amidst the shadows.

"Lady, it's dangerous to have four little kids out this late on this mountain. There are bears and mountain lions in the area, and it's getting pretty cold. Are you lost? I passed you over an hour ago when I drove up the old road on my bike and here I find you still walking down the mountain. Do you need help?"

I was tempted to throw my arms around his neck. "We live near here, but we evidently took the wrong trail, and it has been more than seven hours since we left home. We have been walking down this road for over an hour. My cell phone doesn't work, and I can't call my husband to pick us up. Can you help us?"

The concerned man informed us that he lived only five miles from this point. "Wait for me right here, and I will go home and get my Jeep and come back to pick all of you up."

Obviously, it didn't take me long to consider his offer. Staying on the dark, cold, deserted mountain in the company of coyotes, bears, and mountain lions seemed far more dangerous than trusting our lives to my new, bearded friend.

"Great," we all answered simultaneously, with a few prayers of thanks to God thrown in. It was only after he left that I remembered that I should have had him call Clay to tell him we were still alive!

Thirty minutes later I sighted a small, four-passenger, all-terrain Jeep careening up the bumpy road. As he opened the passenger door gesturing for us all to climb in, the dog jumped in first, followed by the three older kids who squished into the backseat with their beloved Penny. I placed Joy on my lap in the front seat. Getting the door closed was a feat, but we managed, and everyone began to broadcast our story at the same time.

Turning around on the narrow road that hung tight on the edge of a cliff, though, caused all of us to hold our breath and quiet down. I noticed that the girls had closed their eyes. Finally, we bumped our way down the old road, avoiding as many large rocks and potholes as possible, and then slowly moved in the direction of our home.

Twenty-five minutes later we pulled up to the door of our house. Clay ran outside with a look of worry, curiosity, and relief all rolled into one. He had called the mountain search and rescue squad, but they had not yet returned his call, so he was just glad we were back.

With every muscle aching and parched throats, we tumbled out of our rescuer's car and all began talking at once. Amid groans of tiredness and fits of laughter, we thanked our hero profusely, still supposing he really was an angel sent from God. We were all exhausted, but also renewed in our adrenalin-filled joy at having been rescued and finally being safely back home!

Everyone told Daddy about a different part of the great adventure. Nathan called out above the others, "Hey, Mom, that was so much fun. When can we do it again?" to which all the kids said, "Yeah! Let's take Daddy next time. He'd have a lot of fun."

CB

In hindsight, we are all glad we had the experience of our long trek in spite of the difficulty and strain of completing such an arduous climb.

Over the years since that day, it has become a sort of paradigm of my life as a mom—a grand adventure, filled with great joys and extreme demands—beyond anything I imagined—but worthwhile in the end!

I started my walk of motherhood, about two months before I turned thirty-two, with great enthusiasm and grand ideals. In the same way that our mountain walk demanded much more of me than I had planned or expected, motherhood has required much more of my energy, time, and focus than I ever could have imagined. It also has been much longer and more involved than I ever supposed. Only in the past few years have I come to realize just what a long and challenging walk motherhood would turn out to be.

Our mountain walk had wonderful moments of great memories and pleasures as we breathed in the crisp mountain air and beheld many matchless views of the mountain, clouds, flowers, and vistas of the cities below. Yet it also had many moments fraught with fear, pain, difficulty, and challenges with wild terrain through brush, over rocks, and in the dark. So many moments of not having any idea of which way to go or how to continue, requiring over and over again an endurance I didn't know I possessed.

As a young woman, I looked ahead to the adventure of having my own precious brood of children and idealized all the love, fun, and joy we would share as a family. I even pictured myself as the happy mother of joyful, well-adjusted children. My life as a mom has created countless moments of joy, love shared, deep fulfillment, and wonderful memories.

Yet I also have had times of dark depression, loneliness, and feeling that I couldn't keep going. I have often felt inadequate to know just how to discipline and train my children. Choices about their lives have often been a mystery amid so much parenting advice. What movies are acceptable? What is the best way to educate my children? How do I help them handle peer pressure? How is it possible to build godly character into the very fabric of my children's souls? Why is my child resisting me so much? Does my child need more attention or more discipline? And on and on my questions would go.

Like the walk in my story, I found that I was unprepared for the road, and unaware of the obstacles and dangers I would find strewn on my pathway. Often I felt alone in the midst of the difficulties, and more weary than I had ever dreamed I would be. I felt so many times that I needed a guide, a map, the right resources to make the journey, and help along the way. I needed a companion to walk the road with me and to strengthen and encourage me when I felt so alone and forlorn.

What I often experienced, though, is that I didn't really know anyone I could turn to for help. I had many friends, but very few older moms who were spiritually mature and ready to help younger moms. Many times I sensed I was struggling alone but not having any idea if I was actually going in the right direction. With so many people in my life who had such differing values and who had offered such a variety of advice, I didn't know where to turn for real tried-and-true wisdom.

In the end, my children and I are very thankful that we made the "Great Hike" and might even do it again someday. It was indeed worthwhile. Yet, if I had it to do over again, I would plan and prepare for it with much more thought and foresight. I would make certain to take sufficient provisions, appropriate clothing, some means of protection, and reliable communication. I would travel the path with a more experienced companion. I would take a map.

The more I have studied Scripture, the more I have realized that God designed the role of mother to be one of the most important relationships a child will ever have. How I walk my path as a mother will greatly determine the outcome of my children's souls, relationships, vision for life, and success in their own walks with God. Yet as a young woman, finding my way within the rapidly spreading philosophies of the feminist movement of the seventies, I found myself unprepared and uninformed for how to fulfill God's design through my life as a mother.

However, I did find a way that was sure, and it did provide me with the steadiness and encouragement I needed along the way. It was learning how to walk closely with God—how to pray, how to trust, and how to apply Scripture in very practical ways in my life. As I found my way on that path, I began to have the resources for completing this journey well. I can now see how faithful my dear heavenly Father has been in my life, even though I was too young and limited to always understand the routes along which He was taking me.

03

Each of us has a long road we must walk as a mother. The road is extensive and fraught with adventures, joys, obstacles, dangers, and distractions. How we walk the path before us, though, will determine our success as mothers. It's all about the journey, not the destination.

As I contemplated what this meant to me, I realized the significance of this whole concept of "walking" with God as a mom. No one will have exactly the same walk or journey. Your personality, skills, background, husband, financial status, theological underpinnings, children, health, place of birth and residence, relationships, stresses, and so on will be different than any other mom's. Each of us as a mom will have a unique, individual path to walk. Yet how comforting it is to know that God has known all the details of our personal paths and all of our days from before we were born (see Psalm 139).

There are so many books on motherhood that focus on the how-to issues, and often end up in formulaic philosophies about "how to do it" right. But most of these books, though they offer some wise principles to follow, are too general—they cannot exactly fit my circumstances or tell me how to handle my unique problems and stresses. There is no book or speaker that can inform me about precisely what to do to make the right decisions I need to make as my children's mom.

Many times, during my own years of mothering, I would find myself on my knees before the Lord with a problem, struggle, or dilemma to solve, having come to the end of my own rope. What should I do about my child's asthma attacks? How should I handle my child's loneliness? Tantrums? The family member who causes so much stress? My lack of support systems? The neighborhood kids who seemed to be influencing my children in the wrong direction? My struggles in marriage? My own loneliness? Depression? Moves? Financial problems? My child's disadvantage or disability?

Often I would ask advice from others, but just as often I would perceive that others didn't totally understand my own set of circumstances or relationships, or perhaps they had differing values and ideals. Other times I would find the answers dissatisfying or not applicable to fit my situation. Sometimes the solutions others gave me just produced guilt and made me feel that I was not adequate or perfect enough, not the "good mom" that I wanted to be.

However, as I began to read Scripture more and understand my relationship with the Lord better, I realized that God didn't clearly define every issue of family life or parenting in the Bible. Since I know that God is thorough, good, and providential over each day of my life, I knew that He hadn't just forgotten to put all the rules in His Word.

Instead, I began to understand that even as He asked me to live my life by faith, based on the wisdom of Scripture and my relationship with Him, so He intended me to walk this journey of motherhood the same way. I was to walk by faith, seeking His guidance as I came to know Him and His ways, becoming obedient to His principles, and praying for wisdom. It was about learning to walk each day with confidence and assurance in Him, and patiently resting in His promises, His dependable character, and in His provision.

The word "walk" is mentioned hundreds of times in the Bible. It portrays movement and often pictures the spiritual and moral direction in a person's life. It can also refer to the lifestyle and choices one makes in the progression of life. Walking is a metaphor in Scripture describing our journey through this life, and how we choose to live each day as we move toward our final goal of eternity with the Lord in His heavenly kingdom. The Bible is very precise in telling us how to walk the path of life he has set before us, regardless where it may take us.

But there are also admonitions in Scripture of how *not* to walk. We're told "a fool walks in darkness" (Ecclesiastes 2:14). The thematic opening verse of Psalms says the same positively: "How blessed is the man who does not walk in the counsel of the wicked" (1:1). Paul warns the Colossian believers about the darkness, admonishing them to consider themselves dead to "immorality, impurity, passion, evil desire and greed, which amounts to idolatry." He reminds them that these are the ways they "once walked" before they came to know Christ, but now are to "put them all aside" and "put on the new self" they have in Christ (3:5-11). And it is all still true for us as followers of Christ today: We must intentionally choose *not* to walk in the ways of the wicked.

Jeremiah 2:5 warns us of another way not to walk. He admonishes the rebellious nation of Israel by saying, "What injustice did your fathers find in Me, that they went far from Me and walked after emptiness and became empty?" When we go on a path that is apart from a focus on God and His priorities, we will walk after emptiness and become empty. So many youth that I meet in my ministry define their lives as exactly that—empty. They are on the wrong path.

Yet I found many more Scriptures that were very clear about the positive ways in which God wanted us to walk with Him. These passages helped me understand how I was to walk with Him in the midst of being a mother. God intended me to know Him and love Him, but the ideology He laid out for me was not full of detailed laws that applied to each specific instance of my life. Instead, I began to understand that He provided principles of love and trust, as a friend might use for building a strong relationship. In other words, God intended that I would get to know Him and His ways, that I would ask Him for personal help, and that I would trust Him as my loving Father to take care of my life and my children's lives. I was not to follow a formula, but to live by faith in intimate relationship with Him. I was to learn how to walk with Him as my guide and close companion.

As I have seen God's faithfulness and strength equip me for my own "mom walk," it has given me fresh insight and understanding into my role as a mom. He has designed motherhood to be deeply fulfilling, a means of instruction in my life as a Christian, and His way for me to exercise great influence on my children's destinies. It is only as I have followed scriptural admonitions about my walk that I have discovered the secrets to fulfillment and fruitfulness in my own journey as a mom.

The older I get, the more I have realized that only God sees all the details of my life. Only God has access to the heart and soul of my children. Only God knows and understands the stresses I bear uniquely from my own path of life. Only God has been there in the early hours of the morning, when all is still dark, to know, hear, and understand the struggles and problems of my heart that I have poured out to Him. Only God understands the myriad feelings I have sifted through in my heart.

CB

The success of a woman's walk through her years of motherhood is largely dependent on her walk with God. If she learns to love Him and trust Him and listen to His voice through prayer and Scripture, then she will walk on a path of life that leads to success in God's eyes. It is not about how much we can control our lives and the lives of our children, or how well we can live up to standards our culture has imposed on us. It is not a matter of doing all the right things.

It is all about how well we learn to walk this journey with God, and how well we provide a godly pattern for our children to follow and teach them how to walk their own paths with God. It is about living in the presence of God, resting in His will, walking in His power, and being a part of what He is doing in and through our lives.

This "mom walk" we must journey on as mothers is more than an easy stroll down the lane of life. It is a commitment to live faithfully—to walk with God as our guide, with His wisdom and perspective, and with Him to protect us and strengthen us. It is God's will for us to get to the finish line of our mothering journey without being used up, dried out, spent, or depressed. By following His design, we can finish our walks well. He designed us to walk this path with Him, faithfully and fruitfully.

In the chapters ahead, we will look together at the admonitions from God's Word that show us more clearly how to walk with Him on the path of motherhood. I have described the character and qualities that I believe God will require of us on our respective paths with four words from an acrostic of the word "PATH." I believe God wants us to walk with **P**urpose, **A**ssurance, **T**rust, and **H**eart.

May He bless you with understanding as you read and study for yourself the ways in which God instructs us to walk. May your children and grandchildren be abundantly blessed because of your own faithful walk with the One who designed motherhood. You are part of God's magnificent and strategic plan to fill the world with His followers. Your path—your mom walk—will lead you and your children into eternity with our loving God and Father.

Praying with Faith

DEAR HEAVENLY FATHER *≈ Thank you Lord that you know the way for me to go. You created a path for me to walk that is a reflection of your goodness, and a road to Your blessing. I take Your hand as we make this journey of motherhood together. ≈ Help me understand, though, that motherhood is a long journey. Help me learn to walk this journey with You—always having Your perspective on the journey, knowing that along the path of life with my children I am to teach them and to model to them what it looks like to hold Your hand each step of the way. Help me to understand Your Word, which will give me direction and security along the way. ≈ I offer this journey to You as my life's work. I want You to be pleased each step of the way. I am ready to walk with You, to trust you, and to follow wherever you lead me. I want to be a mother after Your heart because I know that You have a heart for me as a mother. I'm ready for my mom walk. ≈ In Jesus' name, I will walk with You. Amen.*

ೞ

Walking by Faith

In the midst of Jeremiah's prophecy of the coming destruction of Jerusalem, God exhorts the people of Judah: "Stand by the ways and see and ask for the ancient paths, where the good way is, and walk in it; and you will find rest for your souls" (Jeremiah 6:16). What does God mean by "ancient paths"? How can your family, in the midst of our own modern times and culture, see the ancient paths "where the good way is" and walk in that good way? How will that bring "rest" to your family?

James, the brother of Jesus, exhorted the new church: "Consider it all joy, my brethren, when you encounter various trials, knowing that the testing of your faith produces endurance" (James 1:2-3). What have been the most difficult obstacles or challenges ("trials") so far in your own journey of motherhood? How have you been able to consider them all joy? How have you grown spiritually because of them?

What can you do to equip yourself in a more strategic way for this long journey of motherhood? Ask yourself: How do I define my journey of motherhood? What are my short-term and long-term goals for my children? What support systems do I need to improve to help me on this journey? (Among other resources, read my book, *The Mission of Motherhood*, for an overview of God's design and plan for mothers.)

CHAPTER ONE

Walking with God on the Path of Motherhood

Yet those who wait for the LORD will gain
new strength; they will mount up with wings
like eagles, they will run and not get tired,
they will walk and not become weary.

ISAIAH 40:31

F inally, I had made it to my seat on the airplane.

I plopped down clumsily, knocking my diaper bag into the lap of a disgruntled man on my right and snagging six-month-old Joel's pacifier ribbon on the clasp of my shoulder bag, which had caught on the armrest on my way down. The pacifier jerked out of his mouth, and Joel, who had finally succumbed to exhaustion and fallen blessedly asleep, began to wail at his rude awakening.

Sweet little three-year-old Sarah just stood next to me holding another bulky overnight bag that had been stuffed to the brim with blankies, picture books, several boxes of apple juice, a Tupperware container of Cheerios, baby rattles and hand toys, an assortment of baby medications, and more. I had tried to think of everything I might need to make the twenty-two-hour flight across the Atlantic ocean and most of two continents as a lone adult with my two little ones. Sarah's big, imploring eyes reminded me that she could not sit down until I relieved her of her excessive burden.

I was en route to America—Texas, to be exact. We were moving back stateside from Austria, and Clay was staying behind for a few days to meet the movers, planning to follow me to America when all the details of our move home were accomplished. He wanted to spare me the hassle of trying to pack and organize with two toddlers underfoot.

This was very kind of him, but the hour-long drive to the airport, the checking of our six massive bags, our foray through security while dragging all of our paraphernalia behind us, and stowing my stroller with toddler and baby in tow had just about worn me out.

The ordeal of flights and changes in airports had not even begun, and I had already expended every bit of reserve patience I could muster as my children tagged along unaware. Shoving the bags into their places while glancing apologetically at my seatmates, I placed baby Joel on the floor on a blanket. We had been assigned the middle, bulkhead seats, smack-dab in the center aisle so that everyone could see us. I fastened Sarah's seat belt and tried to pretend away all the eyes that were focused on our little circus, wondering if we were going to be this disruptive the whole trip. I barely had time to consider the fact that I was really leaving Vienna. After six years in Europe as a missionary with four of them in my beloved Vienna, I hadn't even had time to reflect on my memories or to plan when I would return. All my attention was focused on the present moment of trying to tame and settle my children, and my disgruntled spirit, for the ride ahead.

For the next hour, I tried in vain to get Joel back to sleep. I nursed him, changed his diaper, wrapped him in a blanket and cuddled him, but he seemed particularly fussy. My pediatrician had given me what he called "a mild sedative that will help him to sleep on the plane." He had assured me that he gave it to many Americans who had to make such a flight. Normally I avoid medications unless absolutely necessary, but this seemed to be a necessary occasion. I couldn't imagine wrestling with Joel for the rest of the trip while disrupting the other passengers. Sarah had pushed her three-year-old limits of waiting for my attention as far as she could. Disaster from that direction seemed imminent, so I quietly gave Joel a doze of the medication and hoped for the best.

For the next thirteen hours I juggled, struggled, fumbled, and cajoled my sweet ones through a plane change in Frankfurt, the arduous overseas flight, and customs in New York City. Finally, I was on the last leg of my journey, flying toward Dallas, where Clay's mom would pick me up. A two-hour drive to her home was to end this marathon, but at least we would be out of planes in general and could stop along the way.

I looked down at Joel as he slept fitfully in my arms. He had seemed agitated the whole trip despite the medicine. Though he had fallen into a seemingly deep sleep, he fussed and moaned, tossing his little baby body while he slept. Was it my imagination or was his forehead beginning to get warm? I told myself that it must just be the strain of the strenuous journey. Having not slept for almost thirty hours, I was bone tired and just wanted to sleep. I comforted myself with the thought that when we got to Nana's (Clay's mom's name to all the grandchildren), we could all fall in bed and sleep as long as we pleased.

We finally made it home. Sarah had trooped through the journey fairly well but nearly fell asleep standing up as I pulled her nightgown over her head. Joel, however, had refused to nurse for about the last ten hours and almost seemed to be falling into a stupor. As I changed his diaper and readied him for bed, I saw his little chest heaving with each breath he took. His body was exceedingly warm. When I held him close to me as I rocked him, I could hear a deep wheeze. Dread began to wrap around my heart like a dark blanket squeezing out all light. Something was wrong with my little boy.

What was I to do? Nana lived deep in the Texas countryside, just outside a tiny town of barely seven hundred people. The nearest clinic or doctor was in a town fifteen miles down dark country roads, but it was small and I had no knowledge of the doctors. Hoping that he just had a cold, I cuddled Joel and held him in my arms over the next hour, praying and crying out to God for wisdom. But his little body became more lethargic and limp, his fever climbing higher even with medication, and soon he was gasping for breath.

I needed to act quickly. Nana was asleep by this time and I knew she would have to stay with Sarah. How would Sarah feel waking up in a strange place without me, to a sweet stranger she barely remembered? I made a quick decision to take Joel to the emergency room about fifteen miles away in the closest town. Wakening Nana, I told her what I needed to do and bundled myself and my baby into the car as quickly as

I could. I drove the dark miles in a haze of exhaustion and prayer with Joel gasping for breath at my side.

The doctor who sleepily ushered me into the emergency room did not inspire confidence, but I was helpless and didn't know what else to do. After examining Joel, he looked at me with serious eyes and said, "If you hadn't brought this little boy in, he wouldn't have made it through the night. As it is, it's going to be touch and go. He is getting very little oxygen into his lungs and seems to have some kind of a virus, but it also seems that his body is particularly shut down. Has he received any unusual medication in the past twenty-four hours?" Concern was written all over his face.

I showed him the bottle the pediatrician had given to me. When he found it in a pharmaceutical guide, he glanced at me with alarm. "This," he said decisively, "is not a medication we would ever use for children in America. It was far too strong a dose for such a young child, and I think it has probably shut down some of Joel's system. Combined with the viral respiratory complication, it could prove quite dangerous."

I felt sick inside and a sense of panic and fear swept over me. I had tried so hard to do all the right things. I was so committed to providing the best for my children. I had given my life to them. I had thought I was helping Joel by helping him rest on the long journey. I was following orders of my doctor. What had I done?

The doctor and nurse on call placed Joel on a tall table that had a very flat mattress. He was stripped down to only a diaper. He hardly moaned as they slipped an IV loaded with strong antibiotics into his frail body. The nurse gently attached a patch connected to a tube on his chest, which she told me was a heart monitor. They fitted what seemed to be a small, hard plastic, clear box over Joel that discharged oxygen.

"I'm sorry, but the few rooms we have are full," the nurse said in a matter-of-fact way when she had finished. She looked as though she was tired of emergencies and needed a rest herself. "You can stay with your son tonight, but all we have for you is a chair. It would be best if you could watch him to be sure there are no changes. We don't have any other staff here, and we have to attend to the other patients. Just push the button if you need us."

I wedged myself stiffly into the metal, orange vinyl-clad chair. Picking up a flimsy hospital blanket, I wrapped it snugly around myself. In the warm June Texas night, I was not cold, but I needed something around my shoulders to protect me from the impending feeling of doom I was trying so desperately to resist.

Tears began to flow as much from sheer overload and exhaustion as from sadness. I felt overwhelmingly isolated and alone. Clay was in Austria. My mother didn't even know I was back in America. Nana was asleep with Sarah in another town. I didn't even know a friend I could call. I was sitting by myself in a dark room just barely illumined by the lights on the machines, the only sound the hissing of the oxygen into the plastic tent as Joel struggled to stay alive.

His six-month-old body was stretched out with his arms perpendicular to his sides and his pale, chubby legs extended into a wide V. His eyelids were swollen and red, circled by rings of darkness. Sweat had pasted his straight blond hair to his forehead. His small chest heaved with every breath.

As I watched him, passionate love poured through my fatigued heart. I longed to hold him and rock him and sing to him. I realized how precious this little treasure of a boy was to me. How I wished I could comfort him with life-giving words of hope, strength, and encouragement. How I wanted to pour life into his struggling body.

I wanted so much to have the chance to shepherd him through his life. I had books to read to him and birthdays to celebrate. He had milestones ahead, like walking, riding a bike, learning to swim, learning to read, and running after a ball—moments of life to share together. If only he could know how cherished, how beloved he was.

And yet, he lay there completely unaware of all the love, affection, and compassion that was flowing from my mother's heart toward him. My heart broke into a weak but desperate plea to God for his life, for mercy for my sweet son, for healing from his grave illness. "Lord," I prayed in tears as I watched my baby, "let me know that You are here and that I am not alone. Please help me."

In the first moments after I whispered that prayer and waited, the room seemed a dark abyss, utterly devoid of grace. I found I could barely swallow for the fear that had gripped my heart. But I waited—waited in the darkened shadows yearning for comfort. Gradually, slowly, the darkness of the room began to fade in my mind as I sensed just barely that somehow, even in this despair, I was not alone.

Somehow, I knew in my heart that the Lord was truly with me and caring for my fragile heart. As I waited, as I yearned for His comfort, I began to be aware of answers filling my heart, of comfort coming into my soul in response to my cries. My mind was flooded with thoughts of the Lord, and I suddenly found myself in the midst of a picture of His love and care.

As I watched Joel, it was as if the Lord was saying that He felt the same way about me that I felt about my baby boy: *I love you as you love your son. I created My children to know My love. I wanted to be their companion, their loving Father shepherding them through the seasons of their lives. In the same way your heart reaches out to your precious son, so My heart longs to reach out to each of My children.*

I love you. I am with you. I will never leave you.

Just open your eyes and turn to Me. My love for you is fervent and focused. Sin has created a separation, but I am still here, I will always be here, always reaching out to you in love. Even as you actively love Joel, though he is unconscious and unaware because of his grave illness, so I have loved My children, though their grave illness of sin and rebellion has created a temporary sense of separation from Me. Don't worry. Trust Me. I will take care of Joel. I will take care of you.

That inconspicuous old room, reeking of antiseptic and medicine, whirring with the sounds of the oxygen machine and beeping monitor, became for me a holy place of truly sacred ground. Here, in this unlikely setting, I found my heart filled with worship and thanksgiving. The Lord had engineered, through the seemingly disjointed circumstances of my life, a private meeting with me so that I could understand His love more deeply. In the absence of all the people upon whom I usually depended, in the midst of the chaos of the move, I was ushered into the presence of the one and only person who could help me and who loved me completely. I was brought face to face with the reality of God's love for me and God's love for my child. As my heart was filled with worship, I realized that God loved Joel more than any other person could. Joel was also God's child.

As the night passed I had plenty of time to ponder, and I began to realize that ultimately my children belong first and foremost to God. I am their mother by His design, but He is over all of their lives. I will never really be able to control the outcome or circumstances of their lives no matter how hard I try.

ଔ

God had designed Joel in my womb. He already knew the extent of Joel's days "when as yet there was not one of them" (Psalm 139:16). Joel's destiny is firmly in the hands of the God who loves Him, as is mine. The realization came to me that walking with God through motherhood meant understanding that I, too, am still simply God's child. All of the issues of my life—relationships, circumstances, victories, tragedies, good times and bad, and perhaps especially the intricate tapestry and complexities of motherhood—would be meaningful only as they related to God and His purposes in my life.

He brought me into that little hospital room to be with Him, to know His love, to reflect more on eternity, to see things from His eyes. I thought it was all about my child and my need to provide for him, but really it was about God overwhelming both of us with His care and love. I realized that I was to walk before God in motherhood as I walked in the other areas of my life—with Him as the center of my life, with Him as my strength, with Him as my guide. Like the rest of my life, it was to be a walk of faith and not sight, of believing without seeing.

I would not be able to understand each day or season, or even be able to make life perfect by trying hard. Though I have been given the stewardship of my children's lives and souls, they belong to God just as my life belongs to Him. I am to live it in release to Him, the sovereign God, with peace and faith each and every day.

As I pondered these things, dawn's light began to creep in at the window and my mind jumped to many familiar passages of Scripture. First came the story of Abraham, who worshipped God at an altar upon which he was about to offer the life of his beloved son. Abraham's focus was on loving and obeying God, but he also would have to trust his God completely to provide in a seemingly desperate moment.

At stake was the life of Isaac, his "only son" and the son of God's promise (Genesis 21:12, 22:1-2). In order to test Abraham, God instructed him to sacrifice Isaac. God had called Abraham His "friend," perhaps because his heart was so sympathetic to God and His ways. Abraham's willingness to sacrifice his own son on an altar would become a picture of what God Himself would have to do nearly two thousand years later on a cross of wood. But Abraham could not know that.

All he knew was his son was bound on an altar, and the knife was in his hand. Abraham believed so much in God's love and integrity that he raised the knife to kill his son, knowing that if God asked him to do such a thing, God Himself would provide a way of escape. He had told his companions that he and Isaac "will go over there; and we will worship and return to you" (Genesis 22:5). Abraham's eyes and heart were at peace as he worshipped and rested in God, even in the midst of a seeming contradiction of His character.

Abraham was an example to me in my own motherhood. But even beyond Abraham, I remembered that God the Father Himself had experienced the anguish of watching His own Son die a brutal death on the cross. He knew the torment of a parent watching his child suffer. He knew my feelings about Joel. Yet, God's own Son wasn't saved. He willingly laid down His life so that the entire world could be redeemed back to God through Him.

As I thought and prayed and remembered, my heart was filled to overflowing with knowledge of God's goodness, of His care and love toward His children. I didn't know what God's purposes would be for Joel. This sickness was just the beginning of Joel walking through all the pain and struggles he would experience in life. But I did know I could trust the God who was in charge of the details. In the end both my life and my Joel's life were in His hands.

Peace began to permeate my heart and I felt a lightheartedness seeping into my spirit, driving the heavy darkness away. I didn't have any assurance of what would happen to Joel, but I knew that the One who loved him more than any other would take care of him, whatever the outcome. Later in the day, I drove home to shower and change clothes. Joel was not out of the woods yet, but he was stable for the moment. As I was driving, God brought to mind another verse: "Those who wait for the LORD will gain new strength; they will mount up with wings like eagles, they will run and not get tired, they will walk and not become weary" (Isaiah 40:31).

Again, I contemplated the idea of motherhood. It seemed to me to be a long journey that would take me on many paths yet unknown. But with God as my companion, holding my hand, I knew I would gain new strength for each situation as we journeyed together. He would give me strength for each step of the way to not grow weary or faint; He would invigorate me to be able to run the course and finish with grace.

My part was to choose to place my life and my children into His hands, trusting that He loved me infinitely more than even I love my children. I was to release them totally to Him, knowing that He would take responsibility for them. But more than that, my part was to love Him and please Him daily as I walked this journey with Him, not alone but with His strength, love, and power available to me.

After thirty-six hours, Joel finally awakened fully. He was bright and back to his gentle, playful self with seemingly no repercussions from his terrible ordeal. Yet, I was changed. I had learned a deeper way of walking with my heavenly Father, trusting in His strength as I held His capable hand.

03

My journey through darkness and back into the light of faith with my baby Joel reminded me of a critical truth I needed to know—my life, and my children's lives, are not my own. I am merely God's servant in caring for my children while we are on this earth. They are my stewardship, not my possession. So, as a mother, no matter what my circumstances, I know that I must learn to listen for God's presence, wait for His wisdom, and set my heart on trusting Him completely.

I know that I'm choosing this kind of faith life, not because I'm afraid that God will withhold His hand if I don't, but because I know that it will be what pleases God the most. The author of the book of Hebrews wrote to new Jewish Christians who were tempted to give up on living by faith. Those words are still as true today, for me, as they were for them: "And without faith it is impossible to please Him, for he who comes to God must believe that He is and that He is a rewarder of those who seek Him" (Hebrews 11:6).

My faith is what pleases God, and pleasing God must become the primary focus of my life as a woman, wife, and mother. Faith is the path to my greatest reward from God.

That is a continuous learning experience for me, but when I'm focused on faith in God, I find that I can rest, knowing that even when I make mistakes or seem to fumble through my life, He will be there to pick up the pieces and guide me through each season. Even in my darkest hours and most despairing moments, my life and the lives of my children will be securely in His hands.

This is what it means to walk with God on the path of motherhood—to walk with purpose, assurance, trust, and heart. It means walking with Him as my constant companion, knowing that His love and grace will reach into every corner of my life, and will follow me every step of my way. I will trust God on my journey of motherhood, whatever He asks me to sacrifice or do, because I know He will always be with me to guide, provide, comfort, and inspire me to keep going on my mom walk with Him. And you can take it by faith that he will be there on your mom walk with Him, too.

Praying with Faith

MY DEAR LOVING FATHER 〜 Help me to realize that You love my children as much as I do. When emergencies arise in my life, help me to learn to wait for You, to know Your strength when I am weary, to know Your love in the midst of the dark times. Though I will often be out of control, let me understand that You are always with my children, wherever they are, and that I can ask You to care for them. 〜 You, O Lord, are never out of control, and You will help them in every situation. Help me to see the details of my children's lives as their own story to live out, knowing that You knew "the days that were ordained" for them, even "when as yet there was not one of them" (Psalm 139:16). 〜 I yield my life and my children's lives into Your loving hands. Help me to know how to trust You through each day of my walk as a mom. 〜 I come to You in the precious name of Jesus, Your Son. Amen.

‹⋄›

Walking by Faith

Read Isaiah 40:27-31. God is encouraging His people, near the end of the Babylonian exile, that He is for them, they can trust Him, and He will help them. Do you ever feel like your "way" as a mother is "hidden from the LORD"? Do you ever get "weary and tired" as a mom? When you "wait for" (hope, expect) the LORD, how does that give you "new strength"? How does that help you "walk and not become weary"?

Read Psalm 139:7-12. David declares that no matter where he goes on this earth in his life, God is there with him. He asks, "Where can I go from Your Spirit? Or where can I flee from Your presence?" and answers his own rhetorical questions ... nowhere! Even when light is gone, and he is surrounded by utter darkness and tempted to feel overwhelmed by it, he knows that darkness is not dark to God, and the night is like the light of day. How do these thoughts comfort you in light of all the challenges that will come into your children's lives?

List three specific ways God has been faithful to you in the past. Describe how you can face the challenges along your path of motherhood as you walk it with God's presence in mind. How do the words and examples of Scripture help you stay faithful?

Walking with

Purpose

as a Mother

CHAPTER TWO

Seeking to Please God with All My Heart

Go then, eat your bread in happiness and
drink your wine with a cheerful heart; for
God has already approved your works.

ECCLESIASTES 9:7

Ooh!" shrieked little Joy as she came streaking up the stairs from her basement bedroom. Pounding into the kitchen, she twirled around in excitement. Though it was only five o'clock in the afternoon on a June summer day, she was already clothed in her warmest flannel pajamas.

"I can't wait 'til tonight! I can't wait 'til tonight! I can't wait 'til tonight!"

She sang and twirled to her own very unique song of anticipation as the delights of the night ahead thrilled her to her toes.

Sarah turned around from her post at the kitchen cabinet with a laugh and a glance of huge pride. "Just look at this and you'll get more excited," she said with a flourish of accomplishment as she held out a large basket of giant, dark-chocolate chip cookies.

"Yum! Now I really can't wait. Don't let anyone taste them 'til tonight and then they will be more special," Joy responded.

Four-year-old Joy joined hands with fifteen-year-old Sarah and they both swirled around the room in mutual bliss and giggles until they fell in a dizzy heap onto the couch.

"Hey, you guys, look what we're doing!" the boys yelled from the stairs, determined not to be left out of the preparations or the merrymaking. Joel appeared at the top of the stairs dragging a huge, queen-sized futon mattress up from the basement with Nathan somewhat smothered down below.

"If you three girls would sleep on this together, then there will be just enough foam pads for the boys. Won't Dad be surprised that we did it all by ourselves!"

The boys proceeded to drag the cumbersome mattress across the foyer between the living room and dining room and out onto the wide cedarwood deck. Just at that moment, Clay pulled into the driveway below.

"Hey, Dad! Hi, Daddy!" A chorus of loud welcomes greeted the returning hero of our small kingdom as the four kids ran to greet him, hanging over the edge of the deck to yell their hellos. "Look what we did," the boys yelled as he rounded the last step and surveyed the three sleeping bags and futon all spread wildly and cozily over the end of our deck. The lord of the manor pronounced the work to be of the best sort and then headed indoors to have his hard-earned cup of tea before the grand festivities began.

Since we moved to our mountain home in Colorado, we had made countless memories and had a multitude of crazy adventures. Our house backed up to the national forest, so we had an endless amount of trails and unobstructed beauty to enjoy every day. But at the top of the list of memories made and adventures begun was the discovery that we could camp on our second-floor deck. This was camping in utter ease as it was accessible to bathrooms, the refrigerator, pantry, and, if need be, bedrooms!

Clay's arrival home that night heralded a family campout and picnic on the deck, and the kids were raring for the festivities to begin. I tried stalling them for a few moments with, "It's still three hours until dark, so let's take our time and just enjoy this beautiful night." Instead, they went for a run with the dog to let out their pent-up excitement.

I finished our picnic preparations and surveyed our work with the satisfaction of a queen beholding a beautiful food-laden table in her palace: homemade fried chicken tenders were accompanied by my mom's brown-sugar-bacon-onion-and-liquid-smoke baked beans, deviled eggs, watermelon and cantaloupe, wavy potato chips, and, since tonight's picnic was at home, an added treat of hot buttered corn on the cob. A feast of these proportions was rare in our house, but it was a summer night to be celebrated and we weren't skimping.

The grand finale, to be eaten by starlight, would be the chocolate Texas sheet cake, a family favorite. Why we needed a dessert when Sarah had already made those wonderful cookies I'm not sure, but I gave into peer pressure. "We always have Texas sheet cake when we have our picnics. It's what the Clarksons do." Nathan stated this quite assertively that morning. What could I do but comply?

As I finished up, Sarah came in to get two fat vanilla candles to grace our picnic table, and Joy ran in with a prickly, beautiful bunch of wildflowers to be used as our centerpiece.

"Girls, go find Daddy and the boys and tell them dinner is ready," I directed, as the last hot dish left the kitchen for the waiting table outside.

Clay came out from our bedroom quite refreshed and ready for the party, and Joel came dragging another interesting pile of pillows and an old blanket up the stairs. "We can't leave out Penny—she needs a dog sleeping bag too," he proclaimed with a smile that stretched literally across each side of his face.

The next few hours were filled with a glorious round of laughter, hearty feasting, and games amidst many giggles round the old table. We had a rousing game of Scattergories played out with fierce competition and the kids running in and out of the house and back and forth from the backyard to the deck.

Finally, the sun faded behind the mountain and it was time to arrange the sleeping bags. At seventy-five hundred feet above sea level, the mountain air quickly cooled in the emerging darkness of a summer evening. We all shivered delightedly in the cold and readied ourselves for snuggling up under our multitudes of covers.

Clay's role in our family has always been to be a provider for the details of our lives, so we cheered as he stepped out onto the balcony from our bedroom with an armload of helpful gear and goodies—extra pillows, four flashlights for shining up on the wall and into the sky, a CD player to set the musical mood as we all cuddled in the corner under the awakening stars, and even a box of tissues for runny noses. When we all finally settled down for "lights out," Clay slipped through the screen door behind us into our bedroom to give ease to an uncooperative back that was not suited to sleeping on a deck.

Snuggling in under a gigantic old, fluffy bedspread, the girls and I touched toes and squirmed to find our own private space and get our pillows just right. Sleeping between the restless bodies of my sweet girls would probably keep me awake, but I treasured the intimacy we would have for one more evening—knowing that 15-year-old Sarah, on the cusp of adulthood, might not always be here to share these memories. The boys and dog lined up in a U around us—a boy on each side with Penny at our toes.

We lay in quietness for a few moments. Because we were high up on the mountainside, we were shielded from the city lights below, and we were in awe at the thousands of stars beginning to shine above our humble beds. The cool wind whispered as it blew through the tall pines surrounding our home. The sense of well-satisfied souls was almost palpable as we lay in peace together.

Suddenly, as if to place a final stamp of approval on this celebration of life, a shooting star shot across the dark sky in a blaze of light. "Ohhhh, did you see that? That was amazing. I don't think I will go to sleep tonight 'cause I don't want to miss anything."

Everyone started talking at the same time to proclaim their mutual joy at the small miracle we had beheld.

"I wonder if this goes on every night, and since we sleep inside and don't take the time to notice, we miss so much great stuff," Joel wisely observed.

"All I know is I'm glad I'm a Clarkson and that we can have a party with God tonight," Nathan proclaimed. It became a sort of benediction for the evening as we slipped into a settling depth of sleepiness in our respective corners of the covers. Within moments, only heavy breathing was to be heard all around me.

Yet I was not quite ready to succumb to slumber. I was filled with a sense of deep happiness to be sharing this moment with those I loved the most. As I pondered Joel's statement, I thought and prayed simultaneously.

I don't ever want to take the beauty of life for granted. Thank You for making us a family—our own private club! Thank You for showing Your beauty and love every day. Help me always to take time to notice what You have done and not stay always inside in the darkness, unaware. I love You, my sweet Lord. Thanks for being such a good Father and gracing us with so much pleasure.

And with this as my final thought, I gently shoved each of the girls to their own side of the mattress and contentedly gave in to sleep.

೧೩

In the constant ebb and flow of our lives as mothers, it is all too easy to get caught up in the serious side of our walk with God. We have so much to teach our children: moral standards, an understanding of God's character, prayer and devotions, Bible stories, serving others, manners. It is a never-ending list of light and lessons. Yes, there is a battle for our children's souls so we must protect them. Yes, there are habits of godly cvirtue and haracter we need to cultivate in their lives so we must direct and correct them. Yes, there is so much mother-work to be done. But we also need to realize that there is something much more important to the Lord than all that. In the midst of all our mothering, God wants us to enjoy Him—His presence, His care, His creation, His love. He wants us as mothers to lead our children into celebrating life with Him and taking time to notice the beauty He has provided each and every day. He wants us to revel in His goodness and love.

I was thinking of this lately as I read through the creation story again. I find that Genesis often provides me with an abundance of food for thought in my Christian life. The early chapters of this first book of the Bible contain not only the "in the beginning" of creation, but also some foundational principles to guide my life. Genesis 3:8-9 gave me one very insightful glimpse into the heart of God:

They heard the sound of the LORD God walking in the garden in the cool of the day, and the man and his wife hid themselves from the presence of the LORD God among the trees of the garden. Then the LORD God called out to the man, and said to him, "Where are you?"

God had just completed creation. The trees and flowers, birds and animals, streams and lakes, skies, mountains, and valleys were perfection. The colors—vibrant greens of the grasses and trees, purple of evening sky, red of cherries, marvelous yellows and oranges of fruits, pinks of the flowers—must have been magnificent to behold. The beauty of birds taking flight amid the wild music of their songs, horses galloping, lions lying lazily in the sun, and all the variety of living things that had come from His hand must have brought God great satisfaction and divine joy.

And yet here was God, the One who had created everything out of nothing, calling out for His creature Adam, "Where are you?" Now God knew exactly where Adam and Eve were in the garden, so He wasn't trying to find them. He was looking for their companionship to share in all that He had made for them. He wanted to celebrate, and He wanted to do it with His beloved children. He wanted them to find Him.

As parents, we do the same with our own children. When we have prepared a birthday celebration with food and presents for our cherished children, we enjoy being with them to celebrate together the pleasure we have constructed for their personal fulfillment. Our desire is to see them pleased with what we have provided. We take joy in their joy, because they are objects of our love. How amazing it is to me that above all, God desires and delights in my pleasure of enjoying life with Him, even as I do my own children.

As I have pondered the idea of joyous celebration of life, I always think of David. He is a man in Scripture who seems to have taken joy in celebrating life and worshipping God in the midst of it. In 2 Samuel 6:16, he celebrates the return of the ark to the Israelites, and we find "he was leaping and dancing before the LORD." He continues to offer celebration by sacrificing to the Lord and then distributing cakes of bread, dates, and raisins as he provides "party" food to his people.

We know from other scriptures (for example, 1 Samuel 13:14) that David was a man after God's own heart. David's heart to love and worship God is clearly manifested in the many psalms he wrote to praise God, and to express his love and loyalty to God in every facet of his life. David fervently sought after God, and God responded to him. When his wife Michal made fun of David for dancing so vigorously before the ark, Scripture tells us that she consequently became barren and never had a child from that day on (2 Samuel 6:23). This seems to be pretty important! It seems God was obviously delighted with David and severely judged Michal for her closed and cold heart.

I have always thought it grand that when Jesus was born into this world, God celebrated His birthday in His own celestial way. He created a star just for that occasion that led some of the wealthiest and wisest men to present Jesus with priceless gifts fit for a king. He also showed up with a choir of heavenly angels, who must have sung gloriously as they documented this wonderful occasion for the humble and appreciative shepherds. We see Jesus' delight in providing a glorious celebration for us when we join Him in heaven. In John 14:2-3, Jesus tells us that there are many dwelling places in His Father's house and He is going to prepare a place for us. In His parables, Jesus foretells a great feast which He Himself will prepare for those who belong to Him.

God, the artist, went to great lengths to create tangible beauty for us to enjoy in every facet of life, and to delight our souls. He made visual beauty for our eyes: colors, design, nature. He made audible beauty for our ears: lovely music and song, wind in the trees, rushing waters. He made the beauty of taste and aroma pleasing to our palate: the sweetness of honey, the tartness of lemon and dill, the satisfying aroma of baking bread, the richness of cheese, the bite of chili peppers. We are equipped with tactile senses: touching and caressing other human beings, as well as the soothing comfort of a soft wool blanket or cotton shirt. We have tangible beauty in endless varieties and amounts. There is no end to the number of ways we can take pleasure in God's created world. He provided these pleasures because He loved us.

In the same way, artists find ultimate joy when others can appreciate their creations. When I have made warm cinnamon rolls for breakfast for my family, I feel gratified when they enjoy them, ask for more, and praise me for my cooking skills. So God the artist feels pleasure when we, made in His image and called His children, can appreciate what He has made and praise Him for the delights He has brought us. Amazingly, He longs for our friendship and expresses heartbreaking sadness in the Old and New Testaments when He is ignored and rejected, and His great gifts are left unenjoyed.

The more I have thought about this, the more I am struck by the depth of God's desire for us to enter into the vast experience of beauty which He created. He loves life, and He desires for us to be filled up by His beauty and joy even as we do His work and fight for His ways in a world that does not honor Him. In a way, our obedience of delighting in His beauty is a kind of victory in our daily work and warfare of being followers of God. And where there is victory, there is joy.

As I thought more on this, the Lord brought another precious story to my mind in regard to our ability to bring Him pleasure simply by responding to His proffered love all around us. Mary, the sister of Lazarus and Martha, is remembered throughout the centuries as a woman who seemed to understand what it meant to focus on and cultivate a relationship with Jesus. When Jesus was attending a dinner hosted in their home, Martha was consumed with the duties of preparing the meal. Mary had, for a time, put aside her kitchen duties and cherished the short visit with the Savior. Instead of being distracted by the "doing" of the work of the home, she chose instead to engage her heart with the thoughts and teaching of her Master (see Luke 10:38-42).

Another passage in which this young woman's faith shines as an example to follow was when she wanted to minister to Jesus and show Him her love. She took the costly perfume of pure nard, a whole pound of it, and poured it out on the weary feet of Jesus. She then rubbed His feet with the precious oil, and dried and wiped them off with the soft hair of her own head. This precious perfume was often used by a bride to lavish devotion upon her new husband. It was treasured and saved for a young girl so she would be able to afford such a luxury upon the occasion of her marriage. Or it was bought to use at the death of a relative to prepare the body for burial. Whatever the use, it was very costly, and when it was poured out for another, it was always an action of love showing great esteem for the one on which it was used.

Though Jesus gave His life to serving, healing, having compassion on the downtrodden, and providing for the poor, it is interesting to note His comment regarding Mary's offering in the anointing of His feet. He said, "You always have the poor with you, but you do not always have Me" (John 12:8). He seems to be saying that this time of cherishing Him is important—of stopping in the midst of a normal day of working and serving to take time to love Him and to celebrate His life. It is a way of documenting a moment with Him with an expression of lavish love.

Throughout the Old Testament as well, God instituted feasts for the Jews. They were to stop work and celebrate His faithfulness in their lives. Great preparation was made for them to feast together, sing songs, gather with family, and celebrate. But how does this apply to me as a mother as I seek to please God?

❧

I need to remember that I am to lead my children in what it means to become a person who celebrates the joy of life. I am to model what it looks like to enjoy God and His creation. Often, in the midst of the duties of life, moms can easily become focused only on the right things to do. We can fixate on correcting the immaturity of our children and inadvertently portray God as a strict moral judge just waiting for them to fall short. We can lose sight of God's grace.

It is vital we realize we are a model of God to our children and we must take care that we also present His light, beauty, humor, love, and joy. I love this verse in Proverbs: "A joyful heart is good medicine, but a broken spirit dries up the bones" (Proverbs 17:22).

Though the verse probably applies best to an individual, I have seen how it also applies to our family as a whole. Every day of my life as a mom is filled with chores, duties, problems, issues, and responsibilities. If I allow my soul to become overwhelmed by these things, my spirit becomes dry and depressed, and I pass on my sour and disparaging attitudes—a focus on all that is unjust and hard in my life, the ways my children sin and fall short, a self-centered spirit of complaining and griping My "broken spirit" becomes a virus of darkness infecting every-one else in my house. The only "good medicine" is to choose to have a "joyful heart." No matter what my day holds, I can choose to be joyful.

During a season of some burdensome financial issues in our family, I decided to get up one morning before everyone else. I whipped up some homemade apple-pecan pancakes, lit several candles, put on soothing instrumental music, and had a lovely table set when the kids and Clay came down. We all enjoyed the breakfast surprise together. After the meal, sitting on the couch, Sarah leaned over and kissed my cheek. "You know, Mom," she said, "when you act happy and bring joy to our life, I feel secure and that all is well. But when you are upset and down, I feel guilty, like we have done something wrong, and it makes me feel like brooding. Thanks for making the effort. I feel happy this morning."

I realized that one of the roles God wants me to play in my children's lives is to be a conductor of joy, happiness, and celebration. After all, God designed our need for these things into our very hearts. We were made to enjoy life and our Creator, and we were meant to choose to live in His beauty and provision.

This doesn't mean I won't have difficulties or times of depression. But I do have choices I can make as a mom that will determine the environment in my home. When I choose to notice, every day, the beauty my children display, instead of the duty they bring my way, I am worshipping God. When I choose to notice the gorgeous sunsets and the spring flowers in the midst of busy days, I am teaching my children to dance, so to speak, through their days. When I choose to believe in the goodness of God and verbalize my love for Him, I will make an effort to provide delightful food, thoughtful cards, and moments of fun. I am showing my children a God they will be willing to serve—a God who delights in filling their deep desires for intimacy, happiness, purpose, and beauty.

To neglect enjoying God and celebrating all the wonderful ways He shows Himself in my life is to not really know Him or grow in Him. For at the very core of His character are love, life, beauty, and joy. To know Him is to know and enjoy the pure goodness at the heart of all that He is. To walk with Him is to walk in lovingkindness, pleasure, and delight.

When the Israelites were going from Egypt to the Promised Land that God had prepared for them, spies were sent into the land to see what it was like. Twelve leaders from all Israel made the trip. They did indeed find that the land was flowing with milk and honey. It was filled with abundant fruit and cultivated pastures to be an incredible provision from God—a gift He had planned to give to them. Yet the men also saw that there were "giants in the land," and so they became "as grasshoppers" in their own sight (Numbers 13:33).

Instead of focusing on God's provision and His ability to give them this promised land, ten of the men focused on their fears and what seemed to them like an impossibility. Only two, Joshua and Caleb, reported back to the people of Israel that God would help them to "surely overcome it" (Numbers 13:30).

The Israelites chose to listen to the voice of discouragement, and to reject the wonderful place that God had already prepared for them. They grumbled and complained and even wanted to appoint a leader who would take them back to Egypt—to the land where they had been slaves (see Numbers 14:1-4)! Because of their grumbling and whining spirits, God rebuked the people and condemned them to wander for forty years in the desert wilderness—one year for every day the men had spied out the good land and had chosen not to believe God.

ೞ

What a magnificent lesson this is to us as moms!

There will always be giants in our land. There will always be things that could potentially threaten to overwhelm us. We have to make the choice to believe in God, and in His ability and desire to provide for us. When we do, we will be freed to celebrate His goodness. We can trust Him to lead us into His generous provision, or else we can allow life to demoralize us. If we choose the latter, we will give our children a model of complaining and grumbling, rather than faith and trust.

This story was personally convicting to me, as I do have a real dark side which can become easily focused on the difficulties. However, I have learned an important principle: It is natural to whine and complain or to be selfish and unloving, but it is supernatural to praise and be thankful and to choose to express love and faith. Even when my feelings don't agree, I can choose to live supernaturally.

When we choose to practice praise, joy, and love—when we cultivate celebration even as God did—we then find that we experience the love of God to a greater degree in our own lives. He is there, walking in the garden of our own lives, looking for us to see Him and to respond and walk with Him in His providing love. But in order to see Him, we must turn our eyes and hearts to Him, and seek to listen to Him in our souls. When we do, we validate for our children and ourselves the reality of His joy.

A mother who gives her children a heart to celebrate God's life and beauty gives a gift of life. She is helping her children draw joy from their lives and memories that will bring them strength and pleasure all their days. In the face of so many temptations to become discouraged, Nehemiah's encouragement to the Israelites returning to Jerusalem after their exile in Babylon rings true for us today, too: "Do not be grieved, for the joy of the LORD is your strength" (8:10).

So today, look for joy. Seek out beauty. Model to your children what it means to live in celebration of God's marvelous life. Look for the miracles that go unnoticed each day. Rest in the pleasure of your Lord's companionship and revel in His creation. The end result will be that you bring celebration to the very heart of your own loving Father.

Praying with Faith

DEAR LOVING LORD ❧ You are the Creator of all that is beautiful and good. Help me to celebrate life in its fullness each moment of each day. Open my eyes to see the beauty of Your artistry as I am walking with my children. Let me enjoy with them the softness of the summer grass, the beauty of snowflakes falling on our eyelashes, and the delight of warm cocoa with melted marshmallows on a cold winter's night. When I am on the freeway in piled-up traffic, help me to notice the colors of the sunset. When I am cleaning up messes all around, let me see the beauty of the sweet children who are living in the fullness of life in my home. ❧ Help me to remember that children were made to play and marvel and laugh, and let me learn to participate fully with them every day. Thank You for making life a gift to be enjoyed. I love You, delight in You, and appreciate You today. ❧ In Jesus' name, my Creator of the universe, I come to You. Amen.

౫

Walking by Faith

Proverbs 17:22 tells us, "A joyful heart is good medicine, but a broken spirit dries up the bones." In what way is this true in the lives of your children? How do they feel and react when you are grouchy, angry, or act out depressive thoughts? In what way is a good laugh or a rousing game medicine to your children's hearts?

Name each of your children by their spirit ("Sarah, the spirit of beauty"). Determine one thing you can do with each child that will bring particular delight to their unique spirit.

Galatians 5:22-23 reminds us that "the fruit of the Spirit is love, joy, peace, patience, kindness, goodness, faithfulness, gentleness, self-control; against such things there is no law." We can be joyful, not because of law, but because of freedom in the Spirit. Paul goes on to say, "If we live by the Spirit, let us also walk [keep in step with] the Spirit" (5:25). What keeps you from experiencing joy in your daily life with your children? How can you change your life or attitude in order to walk more faithfully, filled with the joy of God's Spirit and living it out before your children?

CHAPTER THREE

Walking with Integrity at Home with My Children

O LORD, who may abide in Your tent? Who
may dwell on Your holy hill? He who walks
with integrity, and works righteousness, and
speaks truth in his heart.

PSALM 15:1-2

Springtime seemed to be exercising her marvelous powers in a most unusual way this particular year. As I drove with Clay to meet with a young couple we knew, I sat in the passenger seat and stared out in admiration. The green on the trees seemed greener, if possible, than the years before. Daffodils had sprung up by the hundreds, their bright petals lasting longer than usual as the world grew warm. Bluebonnets covered whole swaths of meadow, and the crimson brightness of Indian paintbrush splashed its color in almost every field and yard in our area.

Maybe their heightened beauty came from the mere fact that my heart was full of joy and I was ready to see the beauty around me. The springtime vibrancy reflected my own spirit. After many long years of dreaming about starting a ministry that would reach out to encourage, validate, and undergird parents in their divine calling to disciple their children, our ministry was finally getting off the ground and just beginning to fly.

It had been a bumpy and very faith-fueled ride to this place. For almost five years we had lived off our savings and the odd jobs we could collect here and there. We invested all our money and time into writing books, developing a children's book catalog, and beginning to speak at conferences. We even built onto and moved into the country home of my sweet mother-in-law while we got the ministry up and going.

Our savings dwindled down to nothing in those first years, but dreams are enduring things, and we were tenacious in our struggle to keep our hope in the future and our faith in the God who would bring it. We would spend hours studying our Bibles, praying as fervently as little children, constantly discussing our ideas and then writing down the ideals that came of them. On the more practical side, we shopped at secondhand stores for much of our clothing, made Christmases and birthdays simple (young children can be satisfied with gifts that require imagination, if they've been given one!), and celebrated life with family nights, candlelight, and lots of evenings reading great books aloud.

But finally, after all those meager years and faithful prayers, we had begun to see the hand of God at work in a much larger way in our lives. We had taken a step of faith to rent the ballroom of a local hotel to host our very first WholeHearted Mothers conference—an inspirational conference and weekend getaway to encourage and train Christian mothers to embrace their call to raise their children to be leaders for the cause of Christ's kingdom. The ballroom would hold 650 women. We needed three hundred to attend in order to break even. Oh, how we fervently prayed and asked God to bless us generously, not even imagining what we would do if we had to pay thousands of dollars if no one registered—we didn't have that much money in our bank account!

We sent out brochures to our small mailing list, took out ads in a few newsletters that we knew went to several hundred moms in our area, and posted a few announcements on e-mail loops.

Slowly at first, the registrations trickled into our offices. Our international headquarters were, for the moment, housed in a cramped, century-old farmhouse next door to our home deep in the Texas countryside. The nearby town with a posted population of 716 (which surely must have included dogs as I saw more of them in town than I saw people) had a typically small, understaffed, rural post office.

But at two weeks out, we had three hundred women registered. We were ecstatic—we could now pay our bills! Over the next two weeks, however, the registrations continued to pour in by the hundreds, so that in the end we had to turn people away. On conference day, the ballroom was packed with the sweet faces of 650 young moms whose hearts were eager to celebrate. It was a blessed weekend of fun, inspirational messages, and encouragement as we poured our hearts into what we had long desired to do: strengthen these moms to be the best mothers they could be. Our hearts were all celebration at the end as we reveled in the victory of having seen God provide not just for the conference, but also for our new and growing ministry.

Thus, having just finished the conference the weekend before, I had reason to be lighthearted as we drove along on that spring day. Our years of dreaming and hard work had finally brought us, by God's grace, into a wide place of answered prayer and beginning ministry. The thought of actually earning a salary and expanding this ministry into other parts of the country filled our hearts with excitement. As Clay and I drove to our lunch meeting that day, our spirits were filled with thanksgiving, praise, and profound joy.

The young couple we were meeting for lunch were friends of ours with whom we had been meeting and mentoring for the past year. They loved the Lord and wanted to grow in all areas of their lives so that they could raise a godly family and reach out to others. We had given them some books, provided a free registration to our conference, and prayed with them. We saw so much potential in their lives.

Everything seemed normal as we ordered our salads and filled our coffee cups. But as the young man began speaking, the brightness I had sensed all day began to fade and a sense of darkness seemed to hover over our table. With barely any preliminary comments, the young man began to accuse us of being prideful and self-centered in our success at our ministry conference. When he had finished, his lovely wife began throwing out what felt like poisonous accusations as to our motives for seeking to reach out to so many women and even ascribed attitudes and words to me that I had honestly never felt or said. As we strove to assuage their negativity and reason with them, their voices rose in such bitterness and anger that Clay and I were speechless. We could barely find the words to respond to such a completely unexpected attack.

Becoming literally sick at our stomachs, we ended the luncheon as quickly as possible and almost ran to the refuge of our car. Even when we were alone, we barely knew how to respond to the anger of these former friends. We simply had no resources with which to combat or understand their accusations.

I began to cry, and continued to cry as we reached home and I sought the hiding place of my bedroom. It was as if my heart had been abruptly cut to pieces. To be honest, I cried off and on for the next few weeks. I was shocked that this young couple could feel that way and so misunderstand us, but I was even more stunned that such harsh judgment came from Christians who considered themselves to be "speaking the truth in love" (Ephesians 4:15).

∞

That day somehow crushed the joy I had felt. I would tell myself that they were just one irrational young couple, and that there was still so much to be thankful for. Yet there was something about the shattered nature of this relationship that simply broke my heart. I found myself unable to return to that brightness of spirit that had come with such blessedness after the conference. Though I still conscientiously thanked God for the blessing, I felt let down, cheated somehow. In the midst of our beginning joy over the wonderful success of the conference, it was as if disappointment and pain crept in and utterly spoiled it.

So many years of my life had been given to serving God, to being faithful, and to holding on to Spirit-driven dreams that often seemed impossible. Clay and I had worked long and hard to start this ministry. He had spent countless hours designing our purpose statements, putting together an office and staff, working with the paperwork, and writing and publishing catalogs, newsletters, and our first books. With almost no support or encouragement Clay had managed to get the ministry to a place where it could provide us with a living. And I had been beside him.

In an attempt to be faithful even in the small areas of my life, I had begun years before ministering to moms in the only way I could at first–starting Bible and books studies, organizing outreaches, and putting on teas for women. I had served my children, loved and nurtured them, read to them, and taught them about our precious Lord.

But now, to have the joy of ministry deflated by those we thought were our friends broke my heart. It wasn't that I wasn't thankful for God's blessing, but I felt somehow abandoned, vulnerable, as if despite the first victory, we could be hit again anytime, blindsided by unexpected pain. Was there never to be any time of pure rest, of pure joy, where we didn't have to fear struggle or disappointment?

The above incident is only one picture out of other moments in our lives when we have experienced unanticipated darkness. To be honest, I didn't recover quickly from that time. The repercussions of that broken relationship deeply and lastingly affected both Clay's and my lives, and even the lives of our children. But it was through that time that I was brought to a point of understanding the nature of struggle in our lives.

It was during that time of grief that I realized how deeply my heart desires to live apart from difficulties. My expectation had always been that somehow, eventually, we would get to a place where we could finally rest. I had felt that way with the conference, that finally we had reached a point of victory. So something in me was shaken to find that there was still struggle and grief. The more I thought about it, the more I realized that spiritual struggle seems to be constantly, pervasively present, even in the midst of our greatest joys.

The reason I'm sharing this story, though, is not to focus on the struggle itself, but to understand reality and the nature of it and how to find joy in it. If difficulties are going to be a regular part of our lives, then there must be a way to accept them, move beyond them, and even redeem them. Yet how? How do you redeem dark and broken times?

Perhaps a child has rebelled after a lifetime of the parent being faithful and building into their life. Many women have been abandoned in their marriages as their husbands have left after years of the wife's faithful love and service. Couples have been faithful to love and serve God, only to be rejected by family and friends for having dreams and ideals or coloring outside the lines of life. Loving parents face all kinds of issues with children—disabilities, handicaps, life-altering accidents, chronic conditions, and even terminal illnesses.

There are an endless number of painful scenarios like those that have come to each of us in the midst of walking with the Lord and seeking to please Him. Though God loves us and desires to bless us, we still live in a fallen, sinful, and broken world. It's going to be hard, but He has promised to walk this path of life with us, and to help us endure to the end so we can enjoy the reward of his presence.

I know that, and yet I am still not used to going down the road of righteousness and faithfulness, happily and heartily serving God, only to be blindsided by a new challenge to my spiritual equilibrium. What makes those times harder is that it always seems to be an unexpected blow when my defenses are down.

It has taken me too many years, but after many experiences like that, I have come to realize a simple and obvious truth. It is not when I am walking God's path with a minimum of distractions or difficulties, but in the blindside moments, that the character of my heart and life will show most clearly. It is those times that will manifest graphically what I actually believe about God. Those times will be a picture to me, and to my children, either of what it means to doubt and give in to despair, or to believe in Christ and trust that He can redeem all things. It is especially in the hardest moments of life, when the struggle can be blinding, that our children need to see what integrity of heart and life really look like.

☙

So what does it mean to walk in integrity? What does it mean to walk righteously through darkness and struggle as well as through joy?

David asked the same question in Psalm 15:1-2: "O Lord, who may abide in Your tent? Who may dwell on Your holy hill? He who walks with integrity, and works righteousness and speaks truth in his heart."

Who is the model for utter integrity and righteousness? I have been most encouraged in my own walk with the Lord by studying not just Scripture, but by studying Christ. His life was a long story of redemption, salvation, and victory, but it was also a life wrought in the midst of struggle that ended in a violent death. He is my Lord, the God I serve in ministry, the One I follow, and it cost Him everything to bring light into our darkness. He accomplished redemption, but it was by overcoming a world where sickness, wickedness, and selfishness are the rule of thumb.

As contemporary Christians, we so want our life to be like Cinderella's—happily ever after. We want our rewards now! Prosperity and ease of life now! Answered prayers and blessed families now! Peace and tranquility now!

At least I do.

I am a deeply romantic woman, always yearning for a picture-perfect home—fires on the hearth, hearty feasts and laughter, pleasant and gracious conversations, an ambience of beauty and peace. I write about my ideals. I breathe my ideals in the secret moments of my life. I want an ideal marriage where I am adored and appreciated. I want my children to be healthy, happy, obedient, and harmonious. I want strong, loyal friendships and a loving, life-living community. I want an extended family to be close to us and to provide my children with love, support, and lots of godly input. I want there to be money for all the bills, a home that isn't always exploding with messes, time to sit and read a good book, and quietness to ponder life.

These longings are not wrong. Ideals and the desire for beauty are simply the echoes of God's design in our hearts. He was the one who designed the world to be a masterpiece of wonder and life. The yearning for peace, health, and comfort is natural to our souls. It comes from the depths of our hearts where we can still feel and imagine life as God created it to be before the fall, as He meant life to be.

And yet there was a fall.

Our first parents rejected the Father's rule, and Satan became the ruler of this world. Now he is the corrupter of beauty and the destroyer of life and love. He has set his heart against God and, because we are God's children striving to live in His goodness, he sets his heart against us. He actively seeks whom he may devour (1 Peter 5:8). "Knowing that he has only a short time" (Revelation 12:12), the devil is intent on blotting out any record of God's goodness, especially in the lives of those who proclaim Christ to the world. Satan would love to destroy all that is good in life and in God's life-giving people.

Perhaps the first step in understanding and dealing with the struggle and pain that confronts us in life is realizing that they are a result of brokenness and evil. God didn't intend for us to suffer. It is not His desire for us to live in a broken world. But because of sin we do, and in order to enter into God's work of redemption, His ultimate fairy-tale ending, we have to accept the pain as Christ did and work through it to bring redemption.

The world we live in is fallen and corrupted. In striving for ideals, we hold up a picture of what we hope for and we work as hard as we can to bring Christ's beauty back to the world. But we are doing all of this in the midst of brokenness and we know that life will never be as perfect as we desire. But through it all we follow Jesus. He is the visible picture of perfect goodness who came right into the midst of our broken world and set to work redeeming it.

So, back to our verse in Psalm 15: "O LORD, who may abide in Your tent? Who may dwell on Your holy hill?" How does a mother walk with integrity and work righteousness?

We follow the example of God before us. In Genesis 1, we read that in the beginning the world was formless, void, and dark. But God is the Creator. It is part of His divine nature to create and bring forth something new. So He, in His goodness, spoke light, beauty, color, form, meaning, and love into the darkness and void. The very depth of the original darkness was the stage on which God's presence shone with overwhelming creative power. Our physical world began with an act of divine creation that spoke light into darkness.

It is the same in our spiritual world. Into the absolute void of our sinful hearts and broken souls, Christ spoke eternal light and redemption. His light brings us hope. His love redeems us. Into our discouragement, He speaks comfort. Into our shattered relationships, He speaks healing. Into our grief, He speaks solace. What is our role? It is to follow His example. In our turn, and with His grace in our hearts, we partner with Him. Our own darkness is redeemed when we choose to walk in His light. We bring the living, resurrection power of Christ into the moments of our lives. Our children are redeemed and can learn by watching us to see how the Christian life is really lived.

When we are unjustly hurt, we choose to forgive and love unconditionally. Perhaps writing a note of encouragement and commitment to the one who offended us is a way of showing our children how to turn the other cheek. When we feel abandoned, we choose to believe in God's goodness and live in hope. By spending time in His Word, we choose to believe that we are precious to our heavenly Father, regardless of how others have treated us. We learn to live with a hopeful and cheerful attitude around our children.

It is all entirely by obedience—choosing to do what is right and knowing that the feelings will follow. We practice telling the truth. We give back money when someone has inadvertently overpaid us. We ask our children to forgive us when we have wronged them, teaching them humility through a relationship with us. We seek to bow our knee to God's will, even when it doesn't seem pleasant, so they can learn how to bow their will to God. We live out a visible life of the Holy Spirit working through our lives—love, joy, peace, patience, kindness, goodness, faithfulness, gentleness, and self-control.

When I walk in obedience to the Lord, submitting my will to His will, and choosing to live in a mature way, I show my children how to find peace with God. When they become adults and are living on their own, I want them to have a storehouse of memories and examples to draw from for how to face their own problems. I want them to have a picture in their minds of healthy patterns of life from the life-giving example of a faithful and godly mother.

This process is not easy for me. I tend to have a dark, despairing side to my personality. Sometimes it is only after many tears and struggles that I come to the point of hope and a new effort at godly creativity. But I have learned to practice righteousness as a habit in my life, and this has served to keep me moving toward maturity. In that process, my life becomes a picture of redemption in Christ—a picture of what it looks like to live in Christian strength and joy even in the mist of a hard world. When our lives are not characterized by integrity, we begin to show a lack of grace, a lack of redemptive vision, or a failure to model overcoming faith to our children. And they will live the rest of their lives with that picture.

I have a close relationship with a person who has experienced a complete lack of integrity from her mother. When in public with her daughter, my friend's mom puts on a display of affection—showing love and a false intimacy to her children—in order to impress others by their supposedly close relationship. But the children learned to despise such false exhibitions of love because at home the mother didn't nurture or encourage, spend time with, or even help her children to learn healthy habits for life. This produced a powerful bitterness and a lasting struggle in my friend to have any respect for her mother or even to know how to walk in integrity herself.

By God's grace, though (and after years of hard work and choosing to be faithful), I have come to see the positive outcome of seeking to live with integrity before my children as they have begun to respond to the Lord in their own lives.

ભ

Recently, I was on a mission trip with my two daughters to Australia and New Zealand. I had the opportunity to speak twenty-nine times in eighteen days in five different cities. Our trip was incredibly busy, yet we saw the Holy Spirit actively changing lives and hearts as we spoke with people. Unfortunately, just before we were to come home, we were swept up into a torrent of unexpected difficulties. First, our purses were stolen on the last day of our trip. (Out of a locked car just a few hundred feet from where we stood!) We lost our money, passports, airplane tickets, credit cards, and a host of other needed and valued personal things. After a crazy weekend spent at the U.S. Consulate in Auckland in between speaking sessions and Joy being sick, we managed to get home.

No sooner had we arrived than my elderly mom fell and fractured her pelvis and hip, developing a blood clot and a kidney infection. I had to make an emergency trip to Texas to help take care of her. Clay was put out of commission by a ruptured disk, and we were overwhelmed with decisions and details to accomplish in the coming days. At the end of those five hectic weeks, I was exhausted. The kids were sensitive to the circus of our lives, as they had to take up the slack and help more than ever at home.

We sat around one afternoon on our den couches and discussed this interesting process of integrity throughout the crazy times of life. We talked about how we learn to bring light even into this sort of darkness. I loved seeing my kids wrestle with these things and hoped that after all the effort I had put into modeling integrity, they would at least have some idea of an answer. (Please, Lord!) The discussion finally broke up, and we went our separate ways for the rest of the day.

But when I opened my e-mail later that night, it was as if God was confirming how vital it is for me as a mom to model integrity for my children. In my inbox was a glimpse of the integrity I prayed to see growing in their hearts. It was such a sweet fulfillment of the years I had spent trying to follow God both for myself and my little ones.

First, I had a precious handwritten letter from my then 19-year-old son, Joel, who was maturing into a fine young man:

Hey Mom,

I don't have but a minute, but I wanted to remind you of the lyrics of the song by Andrew Peterson that I was telling you about when we were all talking.

The thought behind the song is that when you feel you are surrounded by darkness, just remember that when God was forming the world, it was all dark and void. But when He spoke and said, "Let there be light," that is when the splendor of creation took place. You are made in God's image too. So speak, in God's name, into your darkness, and He will fill it with His light, and His love will be present with you.

Now, Mom, every time that you feel discouraged and darkness is creeping into your life, I want you to read this to yourself and then speak light into the darkness. I hope that will encourage you!

Love,

Joel

The next morning, my twenty-one-year-old daughter, Sarah, sent an e-mail to me with an article attached that she had written about our discussion. The following is a short excerpt:

My family, and every family who follows Christ and seeks to raise children who will mirror His love to the world, is a visible, tangible picture of God's grace. As we are faithful to live holy and purely, loving God and one another, we become the visible evidence of a God who is loving and redemptive. But the sight of this tangible grace in our lives infuriates Satan. His intent has always been to destroy heart-kindling evidence of God's presence. So Satan seeks to bring about as much discouragement as possible into our lives.

The reality of Satan's attempt to sabotage contentment is evident within the life of my family. There have been so many days when my parents and I have wondered why we were left so seemingly alone. We have struggled through discouragement, broken relationships, lost health, and many quiet problems. We have seen Satan's destructive work in the lives of other families around us through discouragement, hardship, and relationships.

But we have never given up.

We have begun to understand that the void Satan creates in our lives can be the starting point for the glory of God. Jesus is made visible and glorious through our lives when His redemption breaks into the darkness. Our family history is a long drama of Christ's goodness breaking into our darkness, overcoming every obstacle and flooding our hearts with grace.

As I watched the ending of the [Easter] play that night, I realized again, so poignantly, that the void is never the end. The void is only the silence before the storm of God's new creation. The greater the void, the greater the glory of the light when it finally invades the emptiness and fills it with beauty. God began our universe by speaking creation into a void. He accomplished our salvation and redeemed us for eternity by sending the Word of Christ to speak resurrection into the void of sin. And now that same drama of redemption is being played out on a small scale in our own lives.

God is the creator of life in empty places. I watched the resurrection scenes and felt the chorus rising in my heart. God fills in, God restores, and God does not leave us alone in the shadows. God's glory is even best seen in void places, His life most evident in its power when there was no life before. He will accomplish redemption, create beauty in our void, and honor love and faith just as He did through the resurrection of Christ. Just as we live the love of Christ, we also live the triumph of Christ—resurrected, victorious, and incomprehensible life right in the very heart of this beautiful and broken world.

These are the things that encourage my spirit when I see that my children have "gotten it" about living a life of faith. Despite my inconsistencies and shortcomings, by the grace of God it seems my children have caught that picture of seeking and trusting Him in the midst of the struggle, and bringing Christ's light into the darkness.

Our lives have been anything but easy, and I have felt at times as though I would never be an adequate picture of integrity to my children. But as I read their letters that morning, I realized that as I strove my best to picture integrity for my kids, God filled in, surrounded, and caught my children's hearts so that they caught the spirit of what I longed to give to them.

By walking with integrity at home, my children received from my life training for battle that they will need, and now I can see that they, in God's strength, have learned how to stand strong.

Praying with Faith

DEAR FATHER OF LIGHT ❧ *Thank you that you are my life and my light. In a dying world, you breathe renewing life. In darkness, you shine with revealing light. Help me to walk with integrity, faith, and faithfulness no matter what life brings to me.* ❧ *Thank You for being a picture of integrity and graciousness in the midst of Your own Son's struggles— unjust accusations, condemnations, and crucifixion. Hold me close to You. When I feel despair, let me always see Your lovely light and love in the innermost places of my heart. Help me to show, by my faith and courage, what it looks like to choose to be resilient in the midst of my own battles. Let my children learn by my example what they will need to do in their lives when they grow up.* ❧ *Most of all, I ask for Your comfort and grace as Your daughter who is always in need of the assurance of her Father's love.* ❧ *I walk in your life-giving light. In Jesus' name. Amen.*

 CB

Walking by Faith

Psalm 151:1-2 describes the person who desires to be in God's presence as one who "walks with integrity, and works righteousness, and speaks truth in his heart." How would you define personal integrity? What does it mean to "walk with integrity" and to "work righteousness"? How can you exhibit faithfulness and truthfulness in the battles of your life, without giving into bitterness, and ultimately unrighteousness?

Psalm 15:2 says that the person of integrity "speaks truth in his heart." What does that mean? What attitudes and beliefs, if any, do you need to change in your heart that could keep you from becoming a person uncompromised by dishonesty or deceit? In what ways do you need to conform your heart to the image of Christ so that you may reflect righteousness to your children?

Proverbs 20:7 declares: "A righteous man who walks in his integrity– How blessed are his sons after him." According to this verse, why should we care about our integrity? How are your children learning from your own model of integrity? What changes, if any, need to be made in your home so that your family is characterized by godly integrity?

CHAPTER FOUR

Choosing the Light Things for My Family

In Him [Jesus] was life, and the life was the
Light of men. The Light shines in the
darkness, and the darkness did not
comprehend [overpower] it.

JOHN 1:4-5

Summer was approaching quickly.

It had been a whirlwind of a year that left me rather out of breath in every aspect of life—spiritually, mentally, and emotionally. I felt myself to be mentally panting after intense weeks of travel, school, and decisions as to how the summer should be spent. Of course, my whole year had felt rather like a sprint with too much time on the road, in addition to my mom's illness and our move. I couldn't remember the last time I had rested for more than an hour or two.

But as we pondered the summer ahead, Clay gave me a glimmer of hope when he encouraged me to take some time off purely for rest and refreshment. Joel and Nathan were already planning to attend a month-long drama camp at the MasterWorks Festival in Indiana. Clay, as a creative songwriter, had also planned on taking the boys to a Christian music conference to expose them to the musical world.

Thus, it seemed that just the girls were left to decide on something exciting but decidedly restful to fill our summer days. We immediately began to daydream (a natural bent in all the Clarkson girls anyway) about where we could go to make a one-of-a-kind summer memory.

The first place we thought of was Prince Edward Island. Anne Shirley, of *Anne of Green Gables*, was one my girls' literary heroines, and we already knew her island to be a delightful place of surpassing beauty. It was a dream come true a few years back when we had been blessed to finally visit the island on a speaking trip. But that quick trip had been altogether too short, so the idea of a longer visit, even if just for a week, was soul captivating.

"Let's go back again and stay there, just us girls!" Joy exclaimed. Those words were the start of what we call the "girls club," our name for the trips and excursions that just we girls take. Those words also signaled the beginning of a definite summer plan. We set to work on plans to make our dream vacation a reality.

Since Sarah is a whiz online, she organized and made arrangements for our flights and reserved the same rooms where we had stayed on our previous trip. Prince Edward Island is the smallest Canadian province, both in population and land mass, but it is a favorite tourist destination. It was settled primarily by people from the British Isles and adopted a lot of the heritage, holidays, and habits of England, including teatime in the afternoons, all of which we love.

Shaw's Hotel, a lovely farm on the northern shore of the island, is the oldest family-owned business inn in Canada (serving guests like us continuously since 1860). It is our PEI home away from home. Nestled between the ocean and a small inlet, the inn sits right in the middle of a constantly changing landscape of water, sky, and pines.

This lovely practice of taking time to pause during the day for refreshment and rest is one of the reasons I so loved coming to the island. It seemed like such a civilized life! After a relaxed tea, the inn was just a five-minute walk through woods, flowers, and blooming bushes to Brackley Beach and the sea. In contrast to American beaches, which are often crowded, expensive, and commercial, we had never found more than a handful of people on this beach at any one time.

After weeks of planning, the girls club packed their bags and boarded our plane. We spent a whole day connecting on planes from Denver all the way to Charlottetown, where our plane would arrive, so our anticipation rose with each mile traveled. With her nose pressed against the plane window, Joy suddenly burst into a torrent of plans and told us her one very special wish.

"I want to take a walk in the moonlight on the beach and make a memory I will never forget. Do you think we can do that?"

"It sounds like a lovely idea," I replied, loving Joy's heartfelt desires myself and thrilled at the thought of the delight to come.

We arrived in the early evening, just in time to be shuttled to Shaw's Hotel for a late but lovely dinner in its wonderful restaurant, and then settled into our room. The water was just barely visible through the dark and shadows outside the picture windows as we gave into sleep. In the morning, we awakened to the sun-drenched beauty of the water in all its blue glory, and traipsed down the stairs like Anne herself to partake of a breakfast feast. Omelets, home-baked bread, island jams, fresh granola, just-made yogurt, and an endless supply of coffee brought back all the delight and luxury we had remembered from before.

We lingered like real Victorian ladies over our breakfast and then took a rambling, windy stroll over the land surrounding the inn. Lupines had sprung up all over the fields, hundreds of them in varying shades of purple and purest white. Pansies were hugging the porch corners of the grand old farmhouse. Our feet waded through velvety grass edged with tulips and irises, and the breeze coming in from the sea was fresh, strong, and wonderfully cool.

We practically breathed health and peace into our lungs and spirits, and I felt almost physically lighter, as if some of the worry and weariness had been lifted up by that wind and simply blown away.

Joy ran in the grass in front of me, dancing and twirling and chasing after the inn's golden retriever. I felt as happy as she was, and we spent the rest of the day, just us three girls, strolling up the beach, sleeping in the sunshine, collecting shells, and just resting. Little did we know, though, that the evening was going to bring us the best surprise of our first beautiful day, for Joy was going to get her wish.

After a sumptuous four-course dinner, we all agreed that this was a night for a long ramble down the quiet beach. Donning beach shoes and slinging our towels over our shoulders, we started for the beach at a brisk pace, eager to make it through the avenue of dark firs and out onto the open shore. As we reached the sandy beach, Sarah led the way to the top of the lovely dunes, the longest dune system in the western hemisphere, that provided a natural barrier between the small highway we had crossed and the vast sea beyond.

We scrambled up the last few slippery steps of the sandy slope and turned our eyes to the ocean just in time to witness one of the most spectacular sunsets I have ever seen. The sky was awash in a rainbow of rich rose light with swaths of purple and blue running all through it, and the sunlight was turning the edges of the sky gold.

The colors of the sun were perfectly mirrored on the surface of the water and its beautiful reflection seemed to sparkle and frolic as the waves playfully licked the shore. It all felt like a delightful divine light show set to the spectacular music of creation. It was the sort of sight you only dream of seeing when you catch hints and glimpses of it in "lesser" displays of creation's glory. We three sat shoulder-to-shoulder in an awed silence, simply soaking in the magnificent beauty.

I wondered in my heart at the way God, the great artist, had chosen to clothe the ending of this day. The vastness of His beauty was so powerfully displayed in the power and grace of His sky. Just looking at it filled us with awe. It was mind-boggling to realize that God was so full of beauty, so brimful of life and goodness, that He would faithfully paint this quiet northern sky for His own good pleasure, whether or not anyone admired the work of His hands.

As I sat and wondered, a verse I had read a few days earlier came to mind: "The Mighty One, God, the LORD, has spoken, and summoned the earth from the rising of the sun to its setting. Out of Zion, the perfection of beauty, God has shone forth" (Psalm 50:1-2).

Certainly, this was perfection of beauty if I had ever seen it, and in light of its glory, everything else seemed smaller, less important somehow. For the moment, our home in Colorado seemed as far away as though it were a distant memory.

The issues I had been dealing with—the responsibilities and demands of life, the petty weariness—had faded into oblivion. Instead, I was immersed in the peace of this magical moment. It completely blotted out the other things as the splendor of creation flooded my heart and the hearts of my beloved girls. We were three kindred spirits there in that moment, feeling the warmth of our bodies as we leaned against each other, caught up together in the mystical spell of the brilliant display of nature before us.

The colors softened gradually, melting into muted pinks and eventually light purple and blues, slowly fading into darkness. We sat in silence, fearing that words would break the spell. Finally, after the chill of a sunless sky swept over our sunburned shoulders, we began to shiver and reluctantly decided to go home. But it seemed that God was not done yet, and had decided to be especially resplendent that evening.

Just as we were slipping and sliding down the sandy slopes of the dunes, we turned to glance back at the last light in the sky. There, to our delight, hanging low on the horizon, was a blazing moon of burnished gold, lighting up the darkening sky so that it was almost as bright as day. Like a lantern in the sky, its reflected light of the sun shone straight upon our path, as though lighting our way as we left its presence. Joy, in a wild ecstasy of wishes coming true, ran down the ribbon of moonlight, laughing and prancing the whole way.

I suddenly felt as if we had been literally immersed in the light and goodness of God. The entire day had been a feast of His kindness in a thousand different shapes. But this evening of tangible light, this symphony of beauty, did something to my heart. Filled it, I suppose, so that I felt overcome with His goodness.

For the rest of the week, I walked in what felt like an aura of His light all around me. The memory of the sparkling sunset and that gorgeous moon filled my thoughts, edging out the worry and exhaustion I felt and filling my soul with the light I had seen. Though there were no words, God had spoken to me through His creation (Psalm 19:1-6).

Our vacation lasted five more days. They were spent in a lovely rhythm of long walks, deep sleep, long meals, laughter, rambles, and flower picking parties. Each day seemed to overflow with goodness. By the time the morning of our departure rolled around, we felt strong and healthy, our skin tanned, our bodies rested. But most of all, our souls seemed to have been filled again. The thought of home, with its many responsibilities and needs, was no longer overwhelming. We had been filled up. We were ready to take life on again and do it well.

But the memory of that one magical evening especially buoyed my soul. I thought of it often on our trip home, the memory of the beauty and that overwhelming light creeping into my thoughts again and again so that there was simply no room for worry on the airplane or in the first crazy days of unpacking. There was only room for thankfulness, for joy in the beautiful memory.

I walked with the memory of that evening for many coming days.

☙

A number of years ago, I had been going through another extremely demanding season of life. Besides the normal needs of a family of six, little Joy had nocturnal asthma that would awaken both of us every night at just about 1:00 AM for long rounds of medicine and steam showers to help her breathe. Our church was also going through a split, and along with the exhaustion I felt from those long nights, there was a sense of pressure and trouble pressing in on all sides.

Now, I am not given to symbolic dreams, and have only had two in my whole life. But during this time, on one of Joy's good nights when I fell deeply asleep, I found myself awake in a dream in which God was talking to me. In my dream, I was sitting in my living room considering all the problems that were in my life and in the lives of those I loved. There were some huge troubles to ponder, many of which seemed beyond any reasonable or easy solutions.

In the midst of this, God came to me, reached out His large hand, and asked me to climb into it. I stepped into the palm of His hand and very slowly and gently He began to take me up into the realm of stars and galaxies. I remember that it was unspeakably beautiful. He then told me to look down to the earth, where I had been stewing and fretting about all the issues in my life. God asked me a single question: "How big do your problems look from up here?"

I remember glancing down, straining to see the earth, much less my little corner of it. My house and the people in my neighborhood were tiny as gnats, so that I could barely even see them. In response to His question, I told the Lord that they appeared tiny indeed.

"Indeed," He said. "That is how big your problems are to me. I want you to have My perspective and know that compared to the issues of eternity, they are tiny. I can take care of them."

Then the Lord gently took me back down to earth and placed me in my living room. And then I woke up and realized I had been dreaming. But the sense of "all is well" was all around me, invading my soul and driving my petty worries into the oblivion where they belonged. Though not a single situation had changed during my dream, my circumstances no longer seemed overwhelming. They no longer had their former potency because they had been so far surpassed by God's presence.

As I reflected on this dream, I understood that my life looked totally different to God, from His perspective, than it did to me from mine. The details and worries of my life seem to loom so large in my days, casting their shadows over my thoughts and my feelings about life. My perspective is so limited and finite, yet it can control me.

But my dream helped me to realize that even the hardest situations to me are simple to God. From His eternal perspective, they are so small. They are not unimportant in the sense that they don't affect my life, but they are small matters for Him to take care of if I will just choose to trust Him. If I will choose to look beyond them to His vast power and beauty overcoming every darkness and trouble, I will be able to live in strength and peace, knowing that all will be well.

My enchanted night of sunset on Prince Edward Island did much the same thing for my soul as that dream did so many years before. It very abruptly shook me out of my narrow fretting over the small issues and troubles in my life and helped me to enter back into the glory of God's reality–His light, beauty, and artistry in my life and in His created world. What is really real in my life are not my problems, but His constant will to create goodness in the earth and in my heart. The troubles and petty things will eventually pass away by His grace and help. But God and His beauty are eternal. His desire is that I should walk through life with my eyes set on His goodness and my heart set on His beauty.

It is the only way to live with strength and grace in this world. It is the only way I have found as a mother to make it through each stage, each sleepless night, each disappointment, each struggle, and still retain a picture of God's goodness always working in my life. It is a way of life. Just as I came home from Prince Edward Island with the memory of that evening present in my heart, returning to it again and again in the midst of stresses, so we choose as mothers to walk through our days, choosing to believe in God's grace in our lives.

We walk in His light.

ඎ

Throughout Scripture, passage after passage, and author after author, speak of God and Jesus as light:

> The LORD is my light and my salvation; whom shall I fear? (Psalm 27:1)
> In Him was life, and the life was the Light of men. The Light shines in the darkness, and the darkness did not comprehend [or, overcome] it. (John 1:4)
> I [Jesus] am the Light of the world; he who follows me will not walk in the darkness, but will have the Light of life. (John 8:12)
> Every good thing given and every perfect gift is from above, coming down from the Father of lights, with whom there is no variation or shifting shadow. (James 1:17)

We know that God's very first act in creating the world, and in fact His very first recorded words, was "Let there be light" (Genesis 1:3). His Spirit hovered over the waters of a formless and void place, a world that was empty, lifeless, and dead, and the first thing God did was to speak light into existence. He brought light into the darkness and called it good (Genesis 1:4). God's nature is to create light in every area. Into the darkness of every kind of death, fear, or trouble, He speaks a new creation of His own light. In the book of Revelation, we are told that God's presence will light up the whole world (Revelation 22:5).

As we consider our theme of walking, and specifically the biblical picture of walking in the light, we find that John, Jesus' disciple, quite simply encourages us to "walk in the Light [of God] as He Himself is in the Light" (1 John 1:7).

Walking in the light is important to the life of every mother. Every single season of a mom's life is personally and relationally taxing. Being a godly mother demands our emotional, intellectual, and spiritual energy. We draw on internal resources to focus on investing love, encouragement, and wisdom into our children's souls. We are called to serve and give to them out of the wisdom we find in our own walk with the Lord. But because the nature of motherhood is always to give out, a mother's mind, soul, and body are always expending resources. If the soul becomes weary, dark, exhausted, and depleted, then she will no longer have anything in her heart with which to serve her children, husband, and friends. There will only be shadows and discouragement instead of enough light to be shared with all those who are close to her.

Something that must be mentioned as well in this discussion of walking in the light is how easy it is to try to walk in false lights—lights that have nothing to do with the eternal love of God; lights that produce no real life. When women strive to walk by the light of media, culture, popular values, or anything else, they can become immersed in a constant round of struggle and stress. Media, for instance, tries to make you think that life can be perfect—perfect body; House Beautiful home of your dreams; stress-free marriage; intelligent, popular, high-achieving children; a fulfilling job out in the "real" world; successful family life at home with a model husband and good kids.

If we follow these false lights, they will eventually fail us and throw us right back into the shadows. The false lights will leave us empty because most of us can never acquire all the material things we desire. Even if we achieve a house beautiful, that doesn't guarantee that friendships will follow, and loneliness in a lovely place can feel futile. And no matter how hard I work, there will always be messes in a house where six lively people live. Our bodies, skin, hair, and tummies will reveal our age no matter how hard we exercise and diet—I know! I have tried it all, and my body still droops and sags with every new child born and every year lived. I also know that my life has limitations. It would be impossible for me to build godly character in my children and to attend personally to their needs while working in a job outside of my home forty to fifty hours a week. I just can't do it all.

After living with Clay for twenty-five years and after counseling numerous women, I know there are no marriages without stress since there are no marriages with sinless people. Enduring with unconditional love and grace is the only way any marriage makes it. Also, it seems that no matter what book I read or how well I discipline, my children will never become perfect—ever! But life goes on.

Much of the discontent we experience comes from being disappointed by unrealistic expectations in life, and from not understanding the true light of God and what it means to walk by it. Walking in His light doesn't mean getting all of our desires met or having a perfect life. Walking in His light means choosing to look at life from God's perspective and to enter into His design and purposes. Walking in His light means we are given the insight to endure and persevere. God gives us the grace to look back and see that He has produced maturity and contentment through the hard circumstances of life. Through His Spirit, He gives us real internal joy, freedom, and self-confidence that isn't dependent on what we think others think about us; we know it's about what God has said about us.

I am now so much more the person I always wanted to be, but I just didn't know what God would have to do to get me here—to empty my life of darkness in order to fill it with His light. His light shines on my deepest desires and I know joy because He is leading my life. I'm thankful I don't always get everything I want or request.

Walking in His light is not simply a means of self-satisfaction. Yet sometimes we are fooled into thinking this. When we are weary and exhausted from the sheer amount of physical labor and energy expended serving our families, we become deeply stressed because we thought life would be easier. We didn't know how much work our children would take or how imperfect our husbands could be. What happened to the Prince Charming whose sole purpose in life was to meet my needs and make me feel beautiful?

I once read that depression is the result of unresolved anger. If this is true, I think that the disappointment of life is unrealized expectations—not being what we thought it would be, and should be. That can easily become a source of anger that leads many precious women to live in depression all the time. Every "what if" and "if only" that is mentally recalled and rehearsed can slowly fill up a pool of bitter waters that will poison the spirit. There may be lots of bad news to fill that pool, but the good news is that it doesn't have to poison you.

That is why walking in the true, sustaining light of God is so vital. It is only by His grace that we can live in a redemptive way—trusting in His provision and care for all the disappointments, gaining His strength and help to make it one more day. His light doesn't make life perfect, but it does make it hopeful. His light can redeem every circumstance and usher us into the reality of His kingdom lived out on earth. God's perfection is always working within a very sinful world.

೮౩

So what does it look like to walk in God's light? I personally think that walking in the light requires me to take time to be in God's presence in quietness every day so I can refuel from the one source of true light. In both instances I mentioned above—my night at Prince Edward Island and my dream—I was taken away for a bit so that I could regain perspective and choose the light again.

Seeking to walk in God's light, for me, means taking a Sabbath as a time each week to put aside work and to enjoy a day of rest and restoration. It means building specific times into my life where I can regain an eternal perspective. It means taking time in relationships to fellowship with others—my husband and my friends—who love me, encourage me, and build into my life. It means taking in God's life so that I have life to give back to all those in my life. It means making time for dates with my husband, and taking the trouble to arrange to see cherished friends who encourage me in my ideals.

Interestingly, walking in the light is not something I can attain by a teeth-gritted effort; rather, it is a choice I make to draw away and be refilled, to seek light, and to choose to walk in it. And it is in those times that I am filled up for living my days well. In those times I seek to see my life through God's eyes, learning what He wants me to learn and knowing that His desire is for me to enjoy life and to celebrate His light every moment. I am refilling my soul's bucket so there will be more insightful nuggets from which my family can draw.

Walking in the light of Christ and His ways requires me to make a commitment to subdue my schedule so that I can take time to refuel and restore. It is recognizing the truth that if, as Romans 12:2 says, God's will is "good and acceptable and perfect," then God has not given me more to do as a mom than I am able to do in His strength. Doing God's will ultimately brings blessings into my life, not burdens. I believe that.

If I am living beyond my means, feeling stretched, dry, and dark, then I need to simplify my life so that I can find time for reflection to be sure that I am walking in His light—holding on to His perspective, being refreshed in His energy, resting in His wisdom, and enjoying the relationships that He designed to be a blessing to me.

A number of years ago I became physically ill because of burning the candle at both ends for too many years. I was quite exhausted, and a doctor told me I would wear out fast if I kept up the pace. He actually confronted me, peering over his glasses into my face and challenging me with, "Do you just want to kill yourself, or are you willing to change some of your priorities?"

It was then I began to realize that no one else was going to take responsibility for my health and well-being. As a mature adult, I needed to monitor my own life and have a plan for rejuvenating my body and spirit. I realized that was the only way to ensure that I would always have a reasonable amount of love, joy, and peace to extend in my home to my precious ones. I needed to own my life.

For me, this meant taking time for pleasure and rest, even if my house wasn't perfectly clean. (Is it physically possible for a house to be clean if there are six people eating, breathing, wearing clothes, and living life within its walls?) Exercise and sleep became priorities over getting everything done. Simplifying my life and cutting out some activities gave me more hours in my day to be at home and to make time for a quiet time every day.

Choosing to make Sunday a family day of rest and relaxation stopped me from working frantically every day just to try to stay ahead.

I am diligent to save money for things that will delight my soul: a meal out with a best friend, a once-in-a-lifetime trip to Prince Edward Island, or even just a cup of Yorkshire gold tea every day in the afternoon in a real china teacup! (Did I forget to mention one little square of dark chocolate each day has made me a lot more spiritual?)

If I didn't get all of my boxes checked off for all that needed to be done by Saturday evening, I just put all my responsibilities in a file in my mental closet, so to speak, and left them there until Monday morning. I cleared half an hour to read a refreshing book or fun magazine. I made time to take walks, to go shopping, to call a friend on the phone, to enjoy the sunsets, and to worship my Creator.

By organizing my life to make time to dwell in the light and beauty of the Lord, everything else seemed to fall into place. I became a happier, more joyful mom, and my children and husband benefited from me taking life as a gift, not as a job or duty to complete. This journey is a marathon, which requires pacing myself and making sure I don't burn out before the end of the race.

This practice of walking in the light, of focusing on the beauty and joy of God all around me, has kept me going through all these wondrous and often bumpy years of motherhood. Of course, it is rare for me to have symbolic dreams or to actually manage to escape for a whole week to Prince Edward Island. But it is the habit of gathering light, of drawing away to focus on the beauty of creation, of filling up my soul so that my focus is on eternal things again, that has supported me through every season of my life.

As I finish this chapter, I'm sitting in my own blue chair after a crazy day and several hours of writing. I have lit a fat vanilla candle, brewed a perfect cup of tea, and opened the windows so that the wind is mingling with the music wafting in from the next room. I am quiet. My senses and my heart are soaking up the beauty around me. My heart is refocusing.

I am walking in light.

Praying with Faith

DEAR FATHER OF LIGHT ❧ Shine Your light and righteousness into my heart and mind today. Flood me with the truth of Your Word and Your way, and refresh and restore my soul. There is so much darkness in my life as I am surrounded by worldly values portrayed through the media, advertisements, movies, and television. There are dark holes in my soul from unfulfilled expectations of how I thought life should be, but is not. ❧ Help me find time to make a habit of basking in Your presence, drinking in the beauty of Your creation, and soaking in the reality of Your Word. Give me rest for my soul, so when others need encouragement, there will be light, righteousness, and peace from which to draw. Make my soul a treasure chest of Your wisdom from which my children may constantly draw. Give me the self-discipline to so order my life that my habits of retreating to Your presence will provide fuel for my demanding and taxing days. ❧ Fill me with the light of Jesus. In His name I pray. Amen.

ɕʒ

Walking by Faith

John says of Jesus in his gospel (1:4-5): "In Him was life, and the life was the Light of men. The Light shines in the darkness, and the darkness did not comprehend it." How is Jesus light to our lives? What kind of life does he offer? Have you made Jesus, not just books about Him, a focus of your reflections and study? How did He live His life in this world that was different from the other people and leaders of His day?

First John 1:7 says, "if we walk in the Light as He Himself is in the Light, we have fellowship with one another, and the blood of Jesus His Son cleanses us from all sin." Walking suggests movement along a path. How can you better walk step-by-step with Jesus in your decisions, thoughts, and manners? How can you choose to walk in God's light, as Jesus is? How can you give that light to your children?

What sources of darkness are forming the values of your family that need to be changed? Who are the models for your children of walking in God's light? What standards do you need to establish in the areas of television and movies that will expose your children to light instead of darkness? What does it mean to live in light of eternity instead of living for today?

Walking with

Assurance

as a Mother

CHAPTER FIVE

Depending on God's Word Every Step of the Way

How blessed is the man who does not walk
in the counsel of the wicked, nor stand in the
path of sinners, nor sit in the seat of scoffers!
But his delight is in the law of the LORD, and
in His law he meditates day and night.

PSALM 1:1-2

My speaking tour ended with a talk at a lovely ladies' tea. The precious moms who attended were quite responsive to my messages and seemed to especially enjoy the civilized atmosphere in which we ended the day. As I sat enjoying my nibble of scone and sip of tea, a young woman came up to talk to me after the other women had dispersed to chat with friends or pick up their children from the nursery. By her demeanor, it was obvious she didn't want anyone else to hear what she had to say to me.

"I feel so confused, and I'm desperately hoping you can help me," she said, diving right in as she sat down. She took my hand and continued speaking in a whisper. "I am a new Christian and I didn't have a very good foundation in life. As a matter of fact, I was just left to myself to discover what I thought was true about life, morality, and values. I made a lot of mistakes and have a lot of emotional scars from the choices I made. When I became a mom, I knew I didn't want my children to be scarred like I was. I want to do a better job with them, but I feel like I am starting this journey of motherhood already miles behind. I have nothing in my background that would show me the way to walk this journey of Christian motherhood." As she talked, I could sense her frustration mounting and spilling out from her tear-filled eyes.

"Because I didn't have my own beliefs," she continued, "I feel that now I am subject to whatever I hear. I will read one book and it says to discipline in a certain way that feels harsh, yet I will try to practice these methods for a while. Then I will hear a speaker or read another book that teaches exactly the opposite but also sounds reasonable. I am tempted to think I have ruined my children and need to go in yet another direction! How is a mom supposed to know what to do?"

She isn't the only one asking. I have had many such conversations and talked to many women who feel the same way. I had a similar conversation during another meeting, this time over a publishing project with a soon-to-be mom. Trying to start some conversation, I asked when her baby was due, as she was obviously very pregnant.

"In eight days! I am so scared," she responded.

"Oh, it will be wonderful. You'll hold your precious little baby in your own arms, and it will be so natural to love her as you nurture her and care for her. You will grow more familiar with her personality and her endearing ways a little bit more each day if you can make some leisurely time to spend with her undistracted. She will learn to respond to you in such special ways. How long do you get to be home with her?" I innocently asked.

"I'll be home a week and then I'll go back to work," was her matter-of-fact response. "I don't want to miss any of my project deadlines."

"Oh," I said. I couldn't help it. "You will be so surprised at how wonderful your baby can be. I wish you could spend more time with her to love and cuddle and sing to her, and get to see her develop and have a smile that is only reserved for you." The mother in me couldn't stop. "Long hours of restful sleep will help your body to get back to normal. You should see if you can get more time off. It's such a special time for you to bond with your precious little girl." I didn't want to overwhelm her with guilt, but I hated for her to miss the chance to focus her heart on this amazing human being that God was entrusting to her.

At this point, she quite abruptly burst into tears. Looking up at me in surprise, both through her tears and the sudden rush of emotions, she said, "You know, I never thought of that! No one has ever given me permission to even think about how sweet it would be to stay home with my baby for a while. We don't need the money. I just thought all mothers should work because my mom always worked and never had time to spend with me. I never thought about what I might miss!"

The conversations I shared with these two sweet women represent the hearts of many women I've met. In the absence of nurturing mothers who would meet their needs and cultivate a close relationship with them, they had never developed a plan or biblical direction that would guide them in their own lives. They had no basis or picture of what it meant to be a "good mother."

Through our years of ministry, Clay and I have coined a phrase: In the absence of biblical convictions, people will go the way of culture.

What we mean by this is that if a woman doesn't develop her own foundational principles of biblical wisdom to guide her through life, she will base her decisions in life upon the relative truths she hears from friends, neighbors, and media. But Scripture is crystal clear about how important it is to turn from the world's counsel. Walking according to worldliness is a recipe for brokenness and disaster.

The apostle Paul was deeply concerned about this for his disciple Timothy. In a very personal letter to his protege, the last letter he would write before his death, Paul urged Timothy to be faithful, and to guard against being tempted to turn away from biblical wisdom:

> Preach the word; be ready in season and out of season; reprove, rebuke, exhort, with great patience and instruction. For the time will come when they will not endure sound doctrine; but wanting to have their ears tickled, they will accumulate for themselves teachers in accordance to their own desires, and will turn away their ears from the truth and will turn aside to myths. (2 Timothy 4:2-4)

Why preach the Word? So people can learn how to discern God's truth and be kept from turning aside to myths. I could see that process in the women I just mentioned. A thousand insistent voices constantly shout in our ears and hearts in this media-driven, "expert"-informed age in which we live. Magazines, television, websites, newsletters, blogs, and newspapers all pour out different perspectives of counsel. We receive advice from the world all day, every day, from every direction.

But we can't listen to these voices just because they are ubiquitous, persistent, and loud. The wisdom that informs our thinking must come directly from the Word of God. We only have to go as far as Jesus to see how essential He considered the Word of God to be. In Matthew 4:4, when Jesus was first tempted by Satan after having fasted for forty days and forty nights, He responded to the temptation by quoting Scripture. He quoted Deuteronomy 8:3, saying, "It is written, 'Man shall not live on bread alone, but on every word that proceeds out of the mouth of God.'"

Jesus knew the truth of Scripture and it was God's words that He quoted to resist and rebuke Satan. Jesus went on to use two other verses to resist and crush the temptations that Satan brought His way. If Jesus fought His own spiritual battles with Scripture, then it must be a good pattern for us to emulate.

The Word of God has become a treasure chest to me, full of precious jewels, gold, and silver—the source of all that has eternal value and worth in my life. In Psalm 19:10, the psalmist declares that God's words are true and righteous, "more desirable than gold, yes, than much fine gold; sweeter also than honey and the drippings of honeycomb."

ᑳ

The Word of God has many uses in our lives as mothers. I will list a few, as I literally would never have made it through my years as a mom without having my Bible close at hand. It was my way to find comfort, to hear God's will for me as a mother, and to gain His help in all I did. As a friend of mine says, "It's hard to yell at your children when you are sitting with a Bible in your lap!"

First, the Word of God gives us guidance, wisdom, and direction to be the mothers each day He wants us to be.

Psalm 119:105 tells us, "Your word is a lamp to my feet and a light to my path." Many times in my life, I would wake up in the middle of the night worrying about my children, Clay, or my family. I would open my Bible and begin reading, and almost always I would find encouragement or instruction about how to trust God or how to handle a situation.

With His words in my heart, I was able to pray to Him and then leave my concerns in His hands.

When I feel puzzled in areas like childhood discipline or other subjects that can be viewed from many different points of view, I look to the life of Jesus to see how He related to His own disciples. Reading the Gospels—Matthew, Mark, Luke, and John—many times over has helped me to store up an understanding and overview of Jesus' life that changes the way I mother my children.

I haven't just read the words of these divinely inspired books; I have engaged my heart and pondered what the words and stories mean. In this way I have gained a basic understanding of the ways of Christ throughout His life, which in turn has given me a pattern to follow in my own life. Because of the time spent reading the stories of Jesus' life, I can observe that He was patient, gentle, humble, and constantly loving as He dealt with others, and especially with His disciples. He seemed to reserve His harsh judgment and strong words for those, like the Pharisees, who were law-oriented without compassion. In this way, I build in my mind and heart a biblically-informed and Scripture-based foundation for understanding relationships and issues in my own life.

Another way I familiarize myself with Scripture is by regularly using a topical or exhaustive concordance of the Bible to guide my reading.

I have used the NASB Open Bible for more than thirty years now. There are many such study Bibles and tools available. I like the Open Bible because it has an excellent section of references with a topical concordance that lists many verses on a variety of subjects. There is one both in the front and back of my Bible. If I want to know about a concept, such as prayer, love, or faith, I just look in this index at all the verses on that subject. I write the references on the left side of a piece of paper. Then, I look up the verses and write out on the right side each verse that is relevant or helpful in my own life at that particular moment. I also keep a journal to write down verses, thoughts, or lessons I learn. This way I store up knowledge that will be useful to me in other situations.

The second way Scripture is useful to us as mothers is to teach us about the God who designed us to be mothers.

The Bible is where God has told us what He is like. We learn what is important to Him by seeing how he dealt with those who loved and served Him, and those who did not. Our whole Christian life isn't primarily about being good or doing the right thing, but rather about having a personal relationship with our God—a love experienced between Creator and creature, Father and child. God's Word is His love letter to us—His offer of a loving relationship with Him.

By spending time in God's Word, we come to know His heart. God longs for relationship with us and honors those who love Him and search for Him. Reading Scripture with a heart to know Him better, and a mind looking for clues as to how He interacts with human beings, has given me a better understanding of how to please Him. I have learned how He deals with others so that I can better understand His work in my own life.

For instance, as I read and ponder the stories of the Bible—the lives of Abraham, Sarah, Moses, Joseph, and David—I see that they all had to wait for many years to see their promises from God fulfilled. It gives me a pattern for being mature. Apparently some things take a long time. I can see that God's timing and ways in the lives of those He has used are different than the ways of this world, and my own. In this world, I want immediate gratification—answer my prayer now! Yet I see that those who were godly had to wait in faith for years, trusting that they would see the faithful hand of God intervene or provide in His time.

Through Scripture I learn that God is greater than I am, and He has His own plan for my life. He has His own ways and is not to be put in a box where I can contain or define Him. He is to be loved, worshipped, and adored just because He is the loving God He is, regardless of what happens in my life. As I study and explore my Bible, I see that my Heavenly Father works in my own heart to conform it to the image of Christ, His Son. He is concerned about my life and heart training, not just the outcome of my self-absorbed prayers.

Hebrews 12:5-6 says, "My son, do not regard lightly the discipline of the Lord, nor faint when you are reproved by Him; for those whom the Lord loves He disciplines, and He scourges every son whom He receives" (see also Proverbs 3:11-12). A few verses later it goes on to say that "God disciplines us for our good, so that we may share His holiness" (12:10). Again, I learn about God through His Word, and I am able to see that He is forging strength and godliness in my heart through circumstances that He uses as discipline in my life. By reading these verses, I come to see that He is a Father who is taking responsibility for the training of my life.

When I see a verse I particularly like or that gives a basic understanding of life that seems important to me, I underline it. For instance, when I was waiting on God for long-prayed prayers to be answered, and had been studying the biblical idea of waiting on God, I was reminded of this familiar verse in Isaiah 40:31: "Yet those who wait for the Lord will gain new strength; they will mount up with wings like eagles, they will run and not get tired, they will walk and not become weary."

This verse gave me courage to keep on waiting. Now, every time I see that underlined verse, I can remember the history of my trust and God's faithfulness, each a continuing story in my life. My Bible is literally covered with underlining because it helps me to get a glimpse of how God has met me through hundreds of ways over the years. I have logged thousands of hours with Him reading and searching my Bible, and it is through those old underlined verses and the little notes beside them that I can see my legacy of faith growing over the years.

Writing in my Bible makes it my personal history book. If there is something I want to pray for in the life of my children, myself, or Clay, I write their name by the verse with the date on which I prayed for them. In this way, my Bible has become an almost living story of God's work in our lives. I recently came across a date and note from twenty years ago when I prayed for another baby after having trouble getting pregnant. Joel was an answer to that prayer, so I had written Joel's name by the verse and date. Now every time I see the verse and my personal notes in my Bible, I can remember God's faithfulness.

The third way Scripture is useful to us as mothers is as our source of comfort and assurance.

The Bible has been my help, my refuge, and my encouragement in difficult times. I have read through the psalms more times than I can count and underlined hundreds of their comforting, reassuring verses. The psalms express the whole spectrum of human emotion—joy, lament, pain, grief, and love. Nearly half of the psalms are laments, prayers to God amid difficulties or trials. The writers often tell God that they can't see Him and don't see the answers to their prayers.

There is so much human experience, human reality, and human emotion in the Bible, and it is all bound up within the story of how real people relate to God. In Jeremiah there are long laments and songs of sorrow over sin and God's discipline. In Hebrews there is encouragement, a sort of heart-strengthening pep talk for the new Hebrew believers that had become discouraged and weary in their walk with God. In John some of Jesus' last words to His own disciples were, "In the world you have tribulation, but take courage; I have overcome the world" (John 16:33).

Knowing that lament, struggle, and sorrow have all been legitimate experiences of the lives of all believers in the past has helped comfort me in my own life during my times of darkness and doubt. Ultimately, though, the reason these stories and words are so poignant to me in those times is because they are given to me by God. It is through His precious Word that He comes to encourage and renew, gently reminding me that I am not alone in my sorrows. His story reminds me that I am part of a company of believers who have strained against futility and darkness in this world. In real life, light and truth seem so hidden and obscure. In these times, God's Word truly is a "lamp to my feet and a light to my path."

08

All of the grace and help I have spoken about in the last few pages has come into my life because of one fixed habit—I walk daily in the Word as a mother.

From almost my first day as a Christian, I have made it a daily priority to meet with God, to read books about Him, and to do in-depth studies of His Scripture. This habit and these times have built an incredible treasury of truth in my heart and soul from which I draw strength for my life. A daily, regular quiet time when I read the Bible, seek His wisdom, and pray to Him for my needs has been the means through which I am able to stay faithful as a mom.

Without this constant coming to Him, my life would be built on a sandy foundation that would be swept out from under me in times of crisis. I have seen this many times in my life. Jesus put this in picture-book terms when He told the story of the kinds of houses we build:

> Therefore everyone who hears these words of Mine and acts on them, may be compared to a wise man who built his house on the rock. And the rain fell, and the floods came, and the winds blew and slammed against that house; and yet it did not fall, for it had been founded on the rock. Everyone who hears these words of Mine and does not act on them, will be like a foolish man, who built his house on the sand. The rain fell, and the floods came, and the winds blew and slammed against that house; and it fell—and great was its fall. (Matthew 7:24-27)

A life built on any foundation other than the Word of God is a life doomed to fall. But if we, as moms, walk this journey with God's Word as our source of wisdom and life, and if we listen to and apply the words of Jesus to our lives, we will indeed have a house (family) that remains standing through the storms and floods of trials and difficulties. We will have a spiritual legacy that will last through eternity.

Recently, I was asked to speak about how I have conducted my quiet times over the years. There is no one way to do it, and I often get distracted from my norm, but I have a pattern I have followed for years.

Because my life is rarely neat and together, I attempt to make my devotional spot a regular place where I can spend my quiet, holy moments resting in beauty and having a sense of civility. This gives a sense of order to the rest of my life, even when the edges of my life are seemingly out of control. Life in our home with four kids, a dog, and people in and out rarely provides composure. Yet when my inner life is composed, my outer life feels manageable.

I cannot always be consistent to have time with the Lord every day. Sometimes I am too tired to get out of bed. Perhaps I stayed up too late with a sick child, talked too long with older children, or just couldn't sleep. Yet having a quiet time is my ingrained habit most days, a ritual to which I always return because it has built a wealth of God's words in my heart, which in turn energizes me to become the best mom I can be.

I wrote the picture below of one of my devotion times from a morning just this week. I especially needed encouragement from the Lord before a very busy time of dealing with some issues with my children, moving my elderly mom from one state to another, and speaking at a conference. Of course, I also faced the daily duties of cooking, cleaning, and taking care of my family. Nothing is ever exactly the same, but this story illustrates the way I have sustained my heart through God's words throughout all my years as a mother.

The morning light of springtime peeked into my window and wakened me earlier than usual. My body was still adjusting to daylight savings. Though just 5:15 AM, I was delighted to have the chance to spend time with the Lord all alone before anyone else awakened. I gingerly tiptoed out of our bedroom and tried to close the door as noiselessly as possible so that even Clay, a very light sleeper, would not stir.

Continuing my tiptoe-march down the stairs and into the kitchen, I reflected how strange it was that even though I didn't have small babies anymore, I still experienced a feeling of dread that someone would wake up early and spoil my time alone. As an introverted, relational being, I found that having time alone to reflect, read, and pray was the life-source to the rest of my day. When I had time to reflect on the issues of my heart, to define my worries, irritations, and feelings, then I could better deal with them.

Having successfully made it downstairs, I filled the electric kettle with fresh water and turned on the switch, listening for the hiss of the heating water. I rummaged around the kitchen drawers, thinking the last place some mysterious person might have hidden the matches. I finally found one box with one match left. Lighting one or two small candles to create ambiance and an atmosphere of beauty as I prepared to enter in to my time with the Lord was a ritual I had developed years before. Somehow, when I established a serene, adult atmosphere, my heart and spirit would align with the surroundings and prepare me to quiet my soul.

I had purchased a small Queen Anne recliner early in my marriage. It was known to all as "Mom's chair" where I would often retreat when I had a few moments to read. In all the homes in our seventeen moves, I would choose to place my chair near a window where I could look out at a place of natural beauty. Mountains, trees, flowers—the scenes changed with each new home, but there always had to be a view of something from creation.

I almost always had my quiet time in this chair. Countless sacred hours of life-changing proportions had been celebrated here as I entered the throne room of the Lord. Small vanilla candles next to the chair flickered on an antique table. I always kept a basketful of a variety of books next to my chair so that I could feed my mind with devotional thoughts from different writers from all over the world and from different places in history. My beloved, worn, red-leather Bible was in the basket, along with a couple of favorite journals. In these journals, I recorded what I was learning, what I was feeling, what scriptures I was praying, and any thoughts that came to mind that I wanted to keep.

The kettle whistled me back to the kitchen, and I poured myself a strong cup of Yorkshire Gold tea into one of my favorite china teacups, reserved just for quiet times. While taking the warm brew in hand, I snuggled into my chair, reclining it to its full position. Between sips, I just rested, allowing my mind to wander through the thoughts on my heart. Eventually, I found myself desiring to enter into a sacred time with Christ, with my soul's best friend.

Though this ritual of preparing my room and mood for my quiet time might seem excessive to some, it is my way to dignify this special time. In a home filled with children, I feel like an adult when I can create my own space and time of beauty and serenity. Even if the other corners of my life are in disarray, this attempt at civility helps me feel I can somehow tame and manage the unruliness.

Every time I begin yet another time of study, I am vitally aware of the legacy of these morning times. I have invested literally thousands of hours at the feet of my greatest professor and teacher, Jesus. His words in my life have made the difference between a wandering and wasted life, and one focused strategically on the issues of eternity. This time is where I receive His strength, wisdom, and direction for all the moments of my life—as a woman, wife, mom, daughter, and believer. It is where Christ meets me daily and shows me His path and His ways, and He assures me of His constant companionship.

෧

I have come to believe that the success or failure of any woman who hopes to build her children into a godly legacy depends to a great degree on whether or not she is spending time in the presence of the Lord and filling her mind with His Word. In this fallen world of Satan's domain, where we are constantly bombarded with worldly ideals and cultural ideas, we cannot hope to be guided into all truth unless we are daily instructed by the Giver of truth. To my mind, it is pretty certain that whether or not a woman invests time with the Lord will ultimately determine what she has to give to her children, husband, and others.

Through the Word of God, we are able to become skillful builders of our children's souls. May we come often to be enriched by the priceless treasures and jewels in God's Word so that our hearts will overflow with life to fill the treasure chests of our children. May our walk be step-by-step with Him, with His wisdom, and with His assurance. Because of our faithfulness to His Word, may our children be rich with His love, wisdom, and guidance for the rest of their lives.

Praying with Faith

GOD OF TRUTH, WISDOM, REASON, AND DIRECTION ᔰ *You are the source of everything that is true about Yourself, this life, and me. Thank You that You have revealed Yourself to Your creatures through Your Word. Our loving Creator has not left us here without instruction and direction.* ᔰ *Make me sensitive and responsive to Your Word and to Your voice. Help me to establish my life on the foundation of Your Word so that when the storms of life come my way, I may stand fast and secure on your truth. Help me develop deep convictions in my children's souls based on the principles of the Bible, so they will have a wealth of truth to help them in living and making decisions.* ᔰ *Give me fresh insight and new understanding of how to apply Your Word to the everyday issues of my life. Help me to establish a lifelong habit of spending time with You, hearing Your voice. Thank You for making Yourself always available to me.* ᔰ *Your Word is Your presence in my life. In Christ's name. Amen.*

ឰ

Walking by Faith

"How blessed is the man who does not walk in the counsel of the wicked, nor stand in the path of sinners, nor sit in the seat of scoffers! *But his delight is in the law of the* LORD, *and in His law he meditates day and night*" (Psalm 1:1-2, italics added). What distinguishes those who are influenced by culture and the standards of the world, from those who are led by God? Are there any changes you need to make to ensure that you have time to delight in God's Word by studying and meditating?

Psalm 119:11 says, "Your word I have treasured in my heart, that I may not sin against You." What does the word picture "treasured in my heart" suggest to you? How can you "treasure" God's word? If you engage your heart and spend time pondering God's Word, how will that influence your decisions and the standards you establish for your children?

Psalm 119:105 says, "Your word is a lamp to my feet and a light to my path." What does that word picture suggest to you? What steps do you need to take in the lives of your children to help them learn to store up the Word of God so that they can have His light on their path? How can you make your family devotions and other times in the Word with your children more "enlightening" for them?

CHAPTER SIX

Praying to the Father for Motherly Wisdom

Come, let us go up to the mountain of the
LORD, to the house of the God of Jacob; that
He may teach us concerning His ways and
that we may walk in His paths.

ISAIAH 2:3

Nine o'clock in the evening is one of my favorite times of day. It marks the beginning of my finishing point. Once I have reached it, I know we have made it successfully through one more day. It means I can soon snuggle under the covers and rest. It's not that I don't love life and my children, but as all mothers know, there comes a time in the day when you need a breather before the next wonderful yet crazy round of living and motherhood begins.

I had finally reached the nine o'clock point on this particular night. It was April twenty-fourth, not an especially important date except for the fact that it meant I had less than a month and a half to finish this book in time for its June first deadline. Tonight I needed to rest, and I needed to rest purposefully! I was more than anxious to close the door on this day as I planned on getting up very early the next morning to attempt to write this chapter for my book. There were several chapters to finish in my next five weeks, and I knew it would take every bit of effort I could muster to turn in a completed manuscript on time.

Thus, nine o'clock found me hurrying ten-year-old Joy through the normal nightly routine of brush-your-teeth-put-on-your-jammies-and-get-ready-for-bed parental directives. I spread the covers over her, prayed our customary "peaceful dreams" prayer, and rose to leave. But Joy had a lot on her little mind that evening. Thoughts, fears, questions, and comments began to pour out of her bubbling thoughts like a rushing stream. She even wanted to talk about the birds and the bees! Not quite the quick and quiet ending to the evening I had hoped for. Children always seem to know intuitively when you need to get to bed quickly and will pick that particular evening for life-changing, late-night chats. (And it just gets worse with teenagers.)

However, I took a deep breath and did my best to receive the intimate thoughts of her heart gently and treat them with the tenderness they so deserve. After all, these issues of life-giving and how she perceived them would influence how well she would be able to embrace God's design for her own life as a woman. I probably wouldn't help the process by hurrying her through these moments, especially as the coming change of little girl to young woman seemed to weigh heavily on Joy's heart.

Joy longed to enjoy the celebration of life with innocence and freedom, to play and run and dance through her days, so she was somewhat fearful of growing up. She had seen many friends of her own age exchange the lightheartedness of childhood for premature sophistication, which translated into "coolness" and a general attitude of sarcasm and resistance to all things innocent and imaginary. Those things didn't look all that fun or lovely to Joy.

In response to her fears, I didn't want to just tell her facts and truths. Instead, I tried to paint a word picture for her of the beautiful design that God had made for her femininity, and for the sweetness of the Lord's plans for her in His rich design of biblical womanhood. This seemed to captivate her imagination.

"He will make you a princess of light," I said. She liked the idea of being God's princess, so for the next little while I strove to give her an idea of what it meant to be a woman who would bring beauty and life into the world and live fully for the glory of God. "But for now," I finished, "the best thing for you to do is to live every day to the fullest. Play, giggle, dream, create, and have fun. You have this gift from God—

the freedom to be a child with no responsibilities—to enjoy for just a while, so make every moment count!"

Secretly, I wished I could make the moments count, and I could be the child with no responsibility again. But as I watched the tension melt from her face, I smiled a motherly smile, and she smiled back as I began to stand up and back slowly away. Catching at my hand, however, she gave me one of her thoughtful looks and began to pour forth a whole new flood of thoughts, seeing as I had so expertly opened up her soul.

Joy had many hopes and dreams to share that night, but the eager smile of her face soon changed and she informed me with a tentative, secretive look that she had something very dark to say. Now her secrets came out. She had been plagued by guilt and fear regarding a terrible picture and headline she had seen on the newsstand in the grocery store. Her nose wrinkled up in real anxiety.

I took one more deep breath, prayed for patience, and then set about soothing her fearful heart, letting her know how cherished her dreams were to me, and answering the innocent questions she continued to ask. God gave me the grace to thoroughly fill her heart with affection and concern for all the issues of her little life. After three older children, I knew that these times of intimacy were a gift that would pass away all too quickly.

"Mom," she sighed blissfully as I finally managed to tuck her under the covers with the feeling that her soul had been greatly unburdened and that I had surely earned a few more jewels in my heavenly crown. "I love you so much. I feel like I give you my problems that feel so heavy and you take them away and then I can go to sleep without worrying so much. Thanks for helping me. I think I can go to sleep now, and I'll even have good dreams!"

"You're welcome, sweetheart. I love you!" I kissed her and quietly closed the door. I glanced at my watch. It had been over an hour since I had begun the usual goodnight routine. The alarm bells of my mental schedule began to ring with urgency, and I renewed my hurry to bed and tucked myself in, willing myself to go to sleep quickly. Joy, however, seemed to have gotten it right when she said I took her fears and worries so that she could sleep. Now I needed someone to take mine.

Even as I strove to rest, my mind was clicking off a mental list of necessary tasks and details to finish tomorrow. I felt a wave of inadequacy wash over my mind as I sought to close out cold, dark thoughts by snuggling deeper into my covers.

Mothers have lots of worries. It's just the nature of motherhood. If moms could hire a professional worry-taker so they could get more sleep, it would be a big business. I certainly would have hired them. I had my list of worries ready—college loans, scholarship applications, cars to buy, car insurance, braces, health forms, medical check-ups, and all the educational issues of children at elementary, middle school, high school, and college age levels. Meanwhile, just ahead was a trip to Oklahoma to pack up my 83-year-old mom, who was very ill, to move her to another state to live nearer my brother.

Because Nathan actually wanted us to help him get his driver's license by his birthday (unreasonable boy!), this meant spending hours each day in the car with him to complete his required driving experience. Next, even more hours would be spent standing in line at the Department of Motor Vehicles. That day was supposed to be a secluded writing day, but it turned into a day when a jewel fell from my crown. I do not walk in the Spirit very well when I am at the DMV for six hours.

Also on my heart was the impending need to purchase a home. We had rented our present residence for the past two years since we had moved back from Nashville in 2004, but we felt that the house was about to explode. We so longed to unload our dozens of stored boxes of books, our china and our kitchen stuff, and favorite pictures that had been stored in the garage for two years.

But the housing market had exploded in Colorado and gone up in price thirty percent in the past few years. With our savings, we couldn't afford a house of the size and quality that would suit our needs with four kids still at home, offices for the three writers who lived there, and the groups and Bible studies that were constantly in and out.

Sometimes I felt guilty that at fifty-three I still didn't have a family home to give to our children as they were beginning to launch into life. A mixture of ideals and caution had prevented us from buying when we had first moved. We'd had only three days to find a place to live because of a pending ministry trip, and the rental house had looked pretty good then. How could we have known that those first months would stretch into two years of unsettled homelessness? It seems there is always something to feel inadequate about.

Two years later, we were ready to look at houses. However, because of Clay's responsibilities, the task of finding a home fell mainly on me at an overwhelmingly busy time in my own life. After viewing houses all day, we would review the best ones together in the evening. My mental list continued to grow, though: finishing my book, homeschooling Joy, feeding and clothing everyone, preparing talks for upcoming speaking trips, and keeping up with my mother (I had made the trip seven times in the year before when she wasn't even as sick as she was now).

As I was rehearsing this list in my mind, I remembered a doctor's appointment for a teen, a dental appointment for another, a failing grade of one of my children in a class, and a counseling appointment for a child with obsessive-compulsive disorder (I asked God often if it was really necessary for two of my children to struggle with OCD). Then, Joel's college applications, and, we needed another car. *The list was beginning to repeat itself!*

Since I was on a grand roll of anxiety, I began to go through the list of the next few weeks' important dates and tasks. On that list were three birthdays—Clay's, Sarah's, and Joy's—which meant deciding what presents to buy, when to go shopping, and how many more batches of cinnamon rolls to make for the birthday breakfasts. Then there were Joy's piano recital, Awana awards night, Nathan's discipleship banquet, thank-you notes to the grandmothers, speaking trips to Dallas and Montana, airplane reservations to make—the list just grew longer.

My original thought burst upon my mind: *You can't think about all of this. You have a book to write tomorrow! You have a house to find soon. Time is running out because the rental agreement is almost up.* My stomach flip-flopped as I reminded myself why I had been so anxious to begin with.

As I was attempting to reel in my out-of-control feelings of fear and anxiety, I realized how desperately I longed for someone bigger than me to soothe my ruffled soul. It seemed that my Joy and I were alike—both of us needed someone bigger, someone more skilled and experienced with the handling of life's problems, to take our fears and show us how to live. I suddenly missed my mother. Where was my person to soothe my fears, kiss me, and assure me that all was well, to tuck me in peacefully after taking all my worries away?

My eyes opened wide in the darkness. There was no chance of sleep, but as I yearned for someone to be a mother to me as I was to Joy, I was suddenly aware of a stream of memories in my mind that seemed to come from out of the blue.

This tradition of being Joy's nighttime comforter is a long one. I suddenly remembered back to when Joy was a just a little girl, about three, when she used to have terrible nightmares that awakened her just before dawn. Often, around 5:00 AM, she would quietly pad into my bedroom, crawl up onto my side of the bed, and snuggle in next to me. Throwing one of her little legs over my back, she would fall fast and deeply asleep. It was precious to feel the warmth of her soft body. She seemed to know that her place was with me, next to me. Just being with me was enough to give her the ease she needed to fall back to sleep.

She never asked permission. She knew that she belonged with me. As a baby who had nursed for two years, she had grown up being comforted by me. Now, familiar with the close affection of snuggling next to my warm body, she felt secure and fell fast asleep.

In the late night darkness of my present night, I was brought back to those sleepy, sweet mornings, and I remembered how vividly alive one of my favorite psalms had become to me during that time:

O LORD, my heart is not proud, nor my eyes haughty; nor do I involve myself in great matters, or in things too difficult for me. Surely I have composed and quieted my soul; like a weaned child rests against his mother, my soul is like a weaned child within me. O Israel, hope in the LORD from this time forth and forever. (Psalm 131)

As I had read this psalm during my quiet time in that earlier season of life, the Lord had given me a picture for what He desired me to do.

He longed for me to keep myself from being involved "in great matters, or in things too difficult for me." Joy, my sweet little baby, had been such a picture to me of what a child I was to God, and how deeply He desired me to wrap myself into His presence, choose to compose and quiet my soul, and fall asleep in His peace and protection, because that was where I belonged.

I had known then that I couldn't possibly figure out all the ways to get everything done or to make them go away by worrying and fretting. Instead, He wanted me to give these matters to Him—to release the responsibilities into His Hands so that He could carry them for me. Then I could go to sleep, worry free, as Joy did. I was to mentally and emotionally take my rightful place next to Him.

It was the same on this night.

It's funny how abruptly your heart can be changed. As I pondered this memory, thought about the words of this psalm, and went over the way it had all come vividly into my mind, I quite suddenly decided not to worry anymore. Turning over, I pulled the covers up close again, and nestled deeply beneath them and into the peace of my own heavenly Father. I mentally named each worry, asked God to take the burden of each one off of me, and then pictured myself resting against Him as Joy had nestled close to me. I pictured Him touching my face and caressing my arm as I left each burden in His able hands. He would be my worry-taker.

With an almost miraculous sense of peace, I finally fell asleep. It was all in His hands now. He would work on my behalf just as surely as I would for Joy. This pattern didn't suddenly come to me in a moment. It was from a habit of coming to Him and learning over and over again that He had walked with me through all the other seasons so that I could now more quickly release the stresses of this season into His capable hands.

CB

I have found that almost every season of motherhood has brought with it an overwhelming amount of worries, duties, fears, and responsibilities that seemed far beyond my capacity to deal with them.

In my younger years there were sleepless nights, child-training issues, ear infections and asthma, moves, and constant demands on my time and body. Later, during the elementary years, were schooling issues, finding good friends, moves, housekeeping, clothes, activities, and a variety of other constantly new problems.

The present season of my life was no different; the worries had just changed shape. Yet, it seemed apparent that I had somehow made it through them all. Though not all of my problems turned out with perfect solutions, I could see that God had used all of those years of living through the stresses with Him for the good in my life. I had become stronger in my capacity to handle more responsibility. I had learned that many of my worries weren't really all that important. I had seen God meet me at every place to walk me through each situation, just as a mother would a little child.

Every mother I know has endless seasons of stress, challenge, and worry, but it is a waste of time to spend energy and hours worrying, fretting, and troubling ourselves about things that we can't make go away. God has already been through hundreds of generations of mothers' problems with their families before hers, and He has planned to be a constant companion through each and every mother's life.

How can we handle all the stress? Only by learning the place of prayer in the daily moments and issues of life.

Prayer is, simply, exactly what Joy did with me that night in her room before bed. She took every fear, every worry, every guilty feeling that plagued her heart and put it all in my hands. And then she expected that I would answer her, comfort her, and help her as she sought my love and guidance.

We are exactly the same with God.

We are the little children coming to Him, giving up our entire souls with every bit of worry, joy, and fear into His committed, capable hands. Prayer gives me constant access to God's presence. It keeps me in relationship with Him as I was in relationship with Joy when she showed me her heart. It is only by prayer that I am able to release my life into my Father's hands and accept whatever comfort and sustenance He offers.

Seeking God and acknowledging Him as my loving Father puts the cares of my life in a larger perspective. It helps me to walk this journey of motherhood with faith and vision, without always being weighed down by the load of my family's needs.

It is a lesson I am still learning. So many times I have acted as though I personally needed to convince God and plead for Him to take care of me. I have acted incredibly as though prayer was my idea! I am a passionate and lively person by nature. Patience is not a natural virtue. I have often have had the feeling that God was very slow, if not altogether too late in His timing in handling all the issues of my life. Yet, slowly, I am coming to realize that He is God in heaven—His ways are bigger than mine; His purposes are not always clear to me.

Like Joy, there are concepts and designs, plans and purposes that are far beyond my young understanding. Yet I have learned that my Lord is trustworthy and dependable. He has led me through paths of life and navigated me through incredibly rocky times. I am still here, intact and able to love Him and love life, but only because of His grace and His provision for me.

I am convinced after all these years that, even as I naturally cared for Joy and her little worries and fears because she was my daughter, so God is infinitely more concerned about my life because He is a perfect Father who loves me perfectly. So how do we learn to "walk in prayer" and keep this trust always in our hearts?

The prophet Isaiah saw a day when all people would say, "Come let us go up to the mountain of the Lord, to the house of the God of Jacob; that He may teach us concerning His ways and that we may walk in His paths" (Isaiah 2:3). Jesus quotes Jeremiah to call that "house," the temple, "a house of prayer" (Matthew 21:13). Peter admonishes us to cast all of our anxiety on God, "because He cares for you" (1 Peter 5:7).

As I ponder these verses, I see that I am meant to go to God moment by moment. It is meant to be a way of life, a constant rhythm of returning to His presence and His help. All the while, I have to keep in mind that this happens only by my choice. I have to choose deliberately to place everything into His hands, and then I have to decide to actually let it all stay there and go to sleep.

In Matthew 8:23-27, we read the story of Jesus beginning a boat journey across the Sea of Galilee with His disciples. In the middle of their journey, a great storm arose that evidently seemed life threatening to the disciples. The boat was "covered with the waves" (verse 24) so that there was certainly a danger of the boat capsizing. However, as the men looked for Jesus, He was asleep. He wasn't a bit concerned that a huge and overwhelming storm was raging all around Him. Finally, when awakened by the disciples' hysteria, Jesus arose and rebuked the winds so that they became perfectly calm.

And then He rebuked His disciples.

"Why are you afraid, you men of little faith," He asked. As much as they loved Him and followed Him, they still didn't understand the totality of God's strength and protection around them, or their place within it. I am often just like the disciples. Yet the picture God gave me that night was of my own need to surrender the storms of my life into the hands of the Father. I need to get what the disciples were missing—that God is in control and I must simply rest in His provision and protection of me.

Of course, even as I say this, it is easy to ask if this is really possible. How do I accomplish this? Practically speaking, am I just fooling myself by playing a mind game of suppression, hiding away from my circumstances and responsibilities, pretending them away with the power of positive thinking: *The storm won't kill me ... the storm won't hurt me ... the storm isn't really there!*

I don't think so.

I believe that many sincere Christians (like the disciples who followed Jesus) have missed out on one of the most important truths of Christianity precisely because of this doubt. I deeply believe that God intended us to walk each moment of our life in dependent prayer, releasing each fear, trouble, insecurity, and pressure into His able hands. We were meant to walk in freedom, not denying the burdens of our lives, but allowing God to carry them for us so that we are free to serve and love Him in fullness of heart.

I know that I can't, by any amount of positive thinking, make even the smallest of my burdens disappear. But as I understand the role of

God in my life, I can listen to Him, respond to His love and power, and allow Him to be responsible and glorified in every moment of my life.

When Jesus was about to be crucified, He knew His disciples would feel the vacuum of the loss of His presence. Yet He had already planned to provide them with His companionship every minute of their lives on earth until they joined Him in His kingdom in heaven. Even as a parent speaks lovingly to His child, so Jesus spoke lovingly to His disciples in the last supper He would share with them before He died:

> I will ask the Father, and He will give you another Helper, that He may be with you forever; that is the Spirit of truth ... [Y]ou know Him because He abides with you and will be in you. I will not leave you as orphans; I will come to you. (John 14:16-18)

Later in His comments to the disciples, Jesus tells them that "the Helper, the Holy Spirit ... will teach you all things, and bring to your remembrance all that I said to you" (John 14:26).

When I accepted Christ, I was filled with God's Holy Spirit. This Spirit literally took up residence in my heart and is present every second of every day to teach me (John 14:26), comfort me (Acts 9:31), pray for me (Romans 8:26), and guide me into all truth (John 16:13). It is by His strength in my heart that I live the Christian life.

☙

How do we partake of His Spirit in our lives? First, as I become familiar with the Bible, Jesus said that the Holy Spirit would bring the things He said to my mind and that He would lead me into all truth.

How perfectly I saw this happen that night! As I lay worrying, the Spirit brought that picture of Joy immediately to my heart, filling me with the conviction that I needed to trust Him. The words of Psalm 131 were God's words in my heart, prompting me to trust Him just as a child trusts his mother, just as Joy trusted me. When I awakened in the middle of the night, and again my worries quickly pushed their way into my thoughts, God's Spirit brought to my mind the passage about Jesus in the storm, and the words from the Last Supper. The Holy Spirit uses

God's Word to familiarize us with Jesus and then He brings passages of Scripture to our minds so that we know how to live.

Joy trusted me with her deepest fears and problems because of our close and mutually trusting relationship. She knew from experience that I had protected her all of her life, that I had provided for her needs, that I had loved and cherished her, and that I had acted for her good. Based on her knowledge of my integrity and my personal care for her, she was able to trust me with her burdens, to release them and fall asleep, knowing that I would be there to give her strength to face whatever life brought her way.

This pattern of trusting is evident in the lives of the disciples. They lived in constant contact and in personal relationship to Jesus for three years. He instructed them and they daily saw the integrity of His life. They experienced His power through the calming of the storm, the raising of Lazarus, and the healing of the lepers and those who were blind. They understood and were individually changed by His patience with them. They knew His forgiveness and unconditional love in tangible, life-changing ways. Consequently, when Jesus returned to heaven, it was these common, everyday, natural men He used supernaturally through His Spirit to turn this world upside down.

Why? Because of living constantly in prayer—walking in continual fellowship with the Jesus they had learned to know and love while He was on earth. They acted on the truth they knew about Him, through a personal relationship with Him. They had to decide, in the secret places of their hearts, to walk by faith in Christ based on their personal knowledge of Him. They acted on what they knew to be true about Him from the relationship they had built with Him.

As a young Christian, I learned to fall in love with the stories of Scripture. I began to learn the truths about God's character—that He was loving, powerful, morally righteous, responsible for His children, a provider for everyday needs, and compassionate. I also learned that He said He would never leave us and that He would be present in every moment of our lives. In every moment of *my* life.

Prayer is not always an active part of my life. There are days and weeks when my life seems to pass in a blur. But as I learn to walk in relationship with God through every circumstance of my life, and learn to spend focused time praying for all that is on my heart, I grow stronger in prayer. I am investing in kingdom issues when I come before His throne and ask Him to bring His power to bear in my life. The amazing thing is that even Jesus went through difficult moments during His time on earth, and He has endless compassion for us as we struggle to trust Him with our concerns. Storms, temptations, battles, and difficulties plagued every step of His ministry, yet He modeled a perfect trust for all of us. The Gospels are filled with examples of His trust in "the Father." He knew exactly what it meant to rest in the Father like a little child. By that trust, He was able to walk in peace and to work the Father's redemption in the world.

And by following the example of Jesus, I can learn to sleep like a child amid all the storms of life, knowing that He is in control of the wind and the roaring seas all around me. I can recall the wisdom of the psalmist who reminds me that "[God] gives to His beloved even in his sleep" (Psalm 127:2). And I can trust His Word that I am always welcome in the throne room of God: "Therefore let us draw near with confidence to the throne of grace, so that we may receive mercy and find grace to help in time of need" (Hebrews 4:16). Amen!

Praying with Faith

OUR FATHER, WHO ART IN HEAVEN ᨦ *Thank You for being my loving Heavenly Father.* ᨦ *Help me to see Your sovereignty over the details of my life. Help me to learn how to yield to You all of the worries, struggles, and pressures of my life. Let me truly learn to have faith that You can carry these burdens and help me through my life's problems. Teach me how to pray so that I may enjoy communion with You. As Your child, let me learn to enjoy simply being with my Father.* ᨦ *Take my children into Your hands and bless them and care for them. Draw them to Yourself so that their hearts will become Yours. Teach me to rest in You, to seek Your face, to have Your peace in my heart, even in the most demanding days, so that my children will see that You are a loving Father, and they will learn how to rest in You.* ᨦ *Thank You for listening to me always and, as a Father, being willing to carry my burdens for me.* ᨦ *I am your child and I love You. Amen.*

Ⳃ

Walking by Faith

"Be anxious for nothing, but in everything by prayer and supplication with thanksgiving let your requests be made known to God. And the peace of God, which surpasses all comprehension, will guard your hearts and minds in Christ Jesus" (Philippians 4:6-7). List any personal concerns that cause you anxiety and rob you of peace. What do these verses say will result from our prayers of yielding our worries to God?

"For we do not have a high priest who cannot sympathize with our weaknesses, but One who has been tempted in all things as we are, yet without sin. Therefore let us draw near with confidence to the throne of grace, so that we may receive mercy and find grace to help in time of need" (Hebrews 4:15-16). How can pondering the life of Jesus help you "draw near with confidence" in prayer to Him? What is a "throne of grace"? In your own experience, how do you find that "mercy ... and grace" give you "help in time of need"?

What keeps you from having time to pray? Is there a friend who can meet with you regularly so you can mutually support each other in prayer for your families? Buy a journal where you can list your prayer requests and regularly record your needs. Be sure to go back and check off the answers and rejoice in how the Lord has worked in your life.

— CHAPTER SEVEN —

Walking with God to Show Light for Others

For we are His workmanship, created in
Christ Jesus for good works, which God
prepared beforehand so that we would walk
in them.

EPHESIANS 2:10

S nuggling under the covers of the queen-size bed they were sharing, Sarah and Joy were trying to warm up in the frigid hotel room. The air conditioner seemed to be overworking, and it made the girls cold and very sleepy. But though I sensed that she was quite tired and needed to rest, Joy's eyes seemed to say that her thoughts were just about to spill out, and I knew from experience that no sleep would come until they were expressed.

It was the night before our annual mothers conference in Dallas. Around a thousand women came each year from all over the United States and sometimes even from foreign countries. The conferences required a large staff of workers, usually made up of a merry group of friends and their children who volunteered their help and gave many hours of hard work to make it a success. An appreciation tea for these wonderful workers had become an annual affair the day before the conferences. It was our delight to serve them lots of delectable treats, give them small tokens to remind them of the theme of the year's message, and pray with them for God to bless the conferences and their families abundantly with His grace.

Over the years, all of my children loved the special preconference meetings and meals. They would catch up with friends from all over the U.S. and play with the children who had become their bosom buddies through the years of working together. Joy had grown up in this conference experience, but she was just becoming old enough to participate as a real worker.

She seemed to cherish being treated like one of the "big kids" and loved participating. As a little girl, she had helped by passing out candy from a basket to the moms who were checking into the hotel. Now, however, she was finally old enough to work at the registration table. She also loved decorating for the thank-you tea and helping serve the women their plates of food.

So tonight, after all the bustle, Joy opened her large brown eyes very wide to make a point, and began to chatter about all she had been storing in her mind. "Mom, I think that was one of the best teas we ever held for our special mothers. Those chocolate-covered strawberries were really yummy. It was fun to be old enough to serve this year. How long have you been doing this?" I began to count the number of years in my mind, but I was interrupted quite suddenly by Joy's next comment.

"And by the way, Mom, why are we the ones who always have to do all the work? I don't remember going to anyone else's mom conference where we just got to sit around and enjoy ourselves. Don't you ever think of just quitting and going on a vacation?"

I had to laugh inside at the familiarity of the question since Sarah had asked the same thing almost verbatim years before. She had been washing dishes after a mother-daughter Bible study that we held in our home for her friends and their mothers. "Mom," she had questioned as she vigorously scrubbed one last pan, "it seems like we always have lots of people over, but I sure wish someone would have us for once, 'cause I would like to have a meal that we don't have to clean up after!"

I must admit that there was a lingering fear that surfaced from time to time in my heart that my children might one day resent the ministry lifestyle that Clay and I had entered before they were born. Yet by that evening before the conference, Sarah, who is eleven years older than Joy, had seemed to blossom and make it through the paths we had chosen, and now her own heart was aflame for reaching others. Though she had been one of my hardest workers, and had put up with long hours, irrational people, and many miles of traveling in our car hauling books, Sarah had somehow developed her own self-image as a young woman with a stewardship to reach out to others. With each new year of conferences, she had grown in competency as a gracious hostess–reaching out to the many people who came our way, learning to engage in conversation, and sharing her own convictions.

Tonight the process was beginning again with Joy, and I sat up to try to shake off sleep because I knew these sorts of conversations were going to play over and over again in her head as she grew up in ministry. Being a family who loves and lives through great stories, I decided to tell Joy a story that I knew would capture her imagination. I told it to her that night, but in my mind it has become a sort of picture to which I can return when I doubt, or my children doubt, to encourage me in what we do. It's the story of "The Good King."

> Once upon a time, there was a mighty and glorious king who had the most beautiful and vast kingdom in the history of the world. This king was noble of heart and considered it his charge to care for each person who lived in his far-reaching empire. He tended all his lands so that they would produce rich crops and abundant harvests. He planted vast gardens and parks lined with beds of roses and paths for children to walk along. He also saw to it that the farmland would be carefully cultivated so that his subjects would have the brightest and tastiest fruits in the world.
>
> This king was mighty, but his heart was rich with love and kindness, and he ruled his land with justice and mercy so that each of his subjects would feel perfectly secure and entirely happy in his realm. He was rich, and full of natural joy himself, but he knew that being a great king meant more than just being happy. To be a great king he knew he needed to provide for his people's joy as well and see to it that they were well protected. This king was the greatest king that had ever lived.
>
> But there was a very wicked man who was jealous of the beloved king. He envied the king's power and was envious of the

love and appreciation bestowed upon the king by those he ruled. The evil man began to plot how he could destroy the great king and take the kingdom for himself. His plots grew thick and dark, and he began to spread evil rumors about the good king that caused many of the people to doubt his goodness. The evil man whispered that the king was greedy and secretly selfish, keeping hoards of riches to himself. Into the ears of the innocent, the evil man whispered that the king couldn't be trusted and didn't truly have the good of the people in his heart after all.

And though it is hard to believe, the people listened to the lies of the evil man. They began following him, changing allegiance from the good and benevolent king, to the selfish and deceiving liar. The kingdom was split in two as people left their king to serve the wicked man. They thought they would get more if they followed him.

But they were wrong, for the evil man claimed their allegiance and then callously treated them like the dust beneath his feet. He also stole their inheritances and made them to live like slaves under constant oppression. The people groaned at their mistake, but it was too late.

Thus began the great war—the battle between the good king and the evil tyrant. For even as his people left him, the good king resolved that he would do whatever it took to bring the precious people of his kingdom back to their true home, so that once again he could care for them. Despite their betrayal, he would heal their wounds and restore them to their original place of blessing.

But the lies of the evil man had grown so strong that they still held the hearts of many people, despite the darkness that now came and the famine that covered the kingdom. The war raged on and many lives were lost. The great king was determined to redeem his kingdom, but it cost him everything. Even the son of the great king was killed in the battle that was to eventually win the war. Yes, the good king won the war. And through it all, he never lost his love for his people, for he gave everything he had to bring them back to his kingdom where he could bless them and take care of them forever.

I finished my tale and let the story sink into Joy's thoughtful brown eyes for a few moments. Then I finished it up with what I had been building toward all along.

"You see, Joy, this is actually a kind of story about God. He is the great king who loves all of us so much. Satan was jealous and wanted to be the king over all the lands. We know that he lied and stole away the allegiance of Adam and Eve. A war for the souls of all human beings started on that day, and ever since God has been working to redeem and restore everyone who would love Him back to His own kingdom.

"But God, like the noble king, has given us a part in the great battle to redeem the world. It is His way to use the people He restored to then go and help restore other people. We, who have been rescued, are supposed to be His helpers in telling others about His great love and His great kingdom.

"God rescued Mom and Dad when we were young and showed us His love. We learned to love Him so much that we wanted to tell others about His love and help them. Joy, God adopted us as His own children. That makes Daddy and me a prince and princess. As His children, we want to help Him take care of His kingdom and His people, because that is what a prince and princess are supposed to do—to help the King rule wisely over His kingdom.

"He told us to go into the world to tell people about His kingdom and bring them home to be His children. So when we host these conferences, we help others to know about our great King and His love, we help them to see that they can be princes and princesses too.

"When our lives on this earth come to an end, they will be measured by how loyal we were to our God, our King, and by how much we helped to redeem or bring back this world to Him. All of His children are asked to be a part of His battle to bring others back to Himself, but only a few really obey. With all your work and our work at the conferences, we are helping you to learn that He has work for you to do to bring others to Him and His kingdom. We are thankful that you help us reach so many of these sweet mommies so they can learn how to teach their children to be workers for the King."

Joy smiled quite happily at me (and finally with a sleepy look).

"Mommy, I love that story. I also want you to know that I am glad that we get to be a family who serves this great King. It made me feel important today when the moms thanked me for helping. I felt like I was a part of something real important. Mostly, I love being a Clarkson. I just want to be sure I get time to go swimming with my friends tomorrow." Joy kissed me and patted my arm, which has always been her way, and was finally ready to go to sleep.

Joy really did say this, but not all of our days in ministry have been so picture-perfect. Often, when my boys were little, they were a handful. They would bring in the luggage of the women and take it to their rooms at the hotels. Compliments and appreciation from the moms always tickled the boys as they shared stories at the nightly round up, but during the hours of the conference, they would become restless. Many times our kids were exhausted and tired of giving up our home and time for others. There have been infamous moments in our family ministry history. One time, a child looked out the window of our house to see a car full of strangers pulling up in our driveway, to which he proclaimed, "Quick! Everyone hide and maybe they won't know we are here!"

Often at the conferences, behind closed doors, I would have to settle petty fusses between my less-than-perfect kids. Sometimes our family was harshly criticized, and often at these gatherings the enthusiastic moms would monopolize my time. There was one day when Joy was a little girl that a small group of women had stopped by our home unexpectedly. They stayed for two long hours while Joy tapped her foot in the other room and glared. Finally, Joy marched into the living room, crawled up in my lap, and took my face between her hands.

"Mommy," she said as loudly as she could at five and with enough gusto so that she would be easily heard in the room full of mothers, "I wish I had a mom that no one wanted!" Thankfully those moms knew how to take a hint with a smile.

My children have had to haul thousands of boxes of books, brochures, microphones, and decorations. Washing endless piles of dishes, cleaning our messy house again, and giving up beds has been a normal part of life in the Clarkson family as we have had literally hundreds of people stay in our home over the years.

This has been stretching for my children in many ways, and it certainly has never been easy. At times they have even been tempted to doubt God because of the bad attitudes of some of these "Christians" who stayed with us, and by whose words my kids felt hurt and abused. Yet now that they are older, I can see that by the grace of God they have all taken up the cause of the King. Their hearts seem to be turned to Him in a willingness to serve. Of course, we still don't know how it will all turn out in the end—I spend a lot of time on my knees for my children's hearts to stay turned in the right direction.

But this is all part of my essential calling as a mom. As mothers, one of our greatest responsibilities is to walk through the days of our lives seeking to love our King and promote His kingdom. One of the primary ways we do this is by teaching our children and modeling for them what it means to be a devoted servant of the King. We show them what it means to enter into the battle and to be willing to serve and give of ourselves. We are the ones who paint them a picture of the great conflict, the great King, and their roles in fighting for redemption.

౪

God has designed all of us with the purpose of being a part of His redemptive kingdom work. Our children's hearts long to be a part of a great cause. Training our children for ministry is at the center of everything we are attempting to do in their lives. Raising children to serve God is not about knowing all the right rules and keeping them; it is about cultivating compassion in the hearts of our children for a lost world, and showing them how they can practically be a part of His plans to reach the world.

This is so important because our children might never hear this if we don't tell them. In the secular world, everyone's attention, especially the media's, is turned on whoever is the most famous or powerful or wealthy. By the world's standards, the call is not to service in the fight for redemption; it is to self-protection and self-fulfillment, just like the evil man in the story.

But from God's eternal point of view, history in its entirety is the story of His people joining in the battle to spread His kingdom, His rule and reign, over all the earth. Our lives will find eternal value in light of what we do to be faithful stewards of God's kingdom message and ministry, and how we bring redemption and freedom to others through our lives. Each of us is given a unique opportunity to live out a story in which we use the moments, money, talents, and relationships of our lives to promote the priorities that are on the heart of the King, the Lord Jesus.

This is what we absolutely must pass on to our children. I want to suggest three keys to unlock the way to pass on the legacy.

First Key: Understanding Our Part in the Story

It is essential that we ourselves understand that great story. We must personally understand God's call on us as His people to be part of redeeming the world back to Him. God chose to put His Spirit into these bodies of flesh, blood, and bone so that we would be His hands, His words, His love, and His forgiveness to the people of this world. I must personally see myself as responsible for reaching others for Christ.

I have heard many pastors preach about how ten percent of the people do ninety percent of the work in the church. I don't know where that statistic comes from, but in my experience it does reflect truth. Many people have simply never internalized or accepted their own responsibility for God's kingdom or their need to seek out the lost. There are a thousand excuses for not being qualified, but Jesus did not pick trained or qualified men to be His disciples. He simply chose those who were willing to respond to His call and then follow Him.

When Jesus looked out over the people of Israel, He had compassion for them because they were downhearted and seemed like sheep without a shepherd. But he turned to His disciples to make them part of His unfolding story and said to them, "The harvest is plentiful, but the workers are few. Therefore beseech the Lord of the harvest to send out workers into His harvest" (Matthew 9:37-38).

Like Jesus' disciples, we are to be those workers. Even more, if we don't take on the stewardship of the world that God has placed into our hands, our children will inherit a world in which it will be incredibly difficult to live fully and in a godly way. If we do not determine to be servants to other people, our children will find it impossible to find like-minded friends or marriage partners, or anyone to share their worldview and love for God. If we desire for our children to have a culture that is moral, righteous, and just, then we must build righteousness and justice into their lives, and work to protect and promote righteousness and justice in our own nation and world.

I believe that because many mothers have gone into the work-force and left their children to be raised by others in schools, neighborhoods, and churches, we are seeing a generation of children who are spiritually lost, amoral or immoral, and they don't understand or believe in the principles of Scripture. I know that many women must work to help sustain their family's income. However, it is essential to find a way to keep the priority of raising our children for God's purposes at the center of our priorities. Decisions have consequences. If work or career becomes so distracting that our children become victims of our neglect—either spiritually, morally, or emotionally—then we will have to answer to God for the stewardship of their lives. God gave parents the responsibility of training, protecting, and providing for their children.

I have no desire to make anyone feel guilty, but I do have a desire to help stir up mothers to understand the needs of their children. I am a working mom as a writer and speaker. However, I have had to juggle the responsibilities of my ministry in such a way as to be sure I am available to my children. I can see the influences vying for their hearts—television, movies, music, social media, peer pressure, voices tempting them away from faith and purity. I need to be there with and for them.

Our children are looking for love, guidance, and affirmation. If they don't have their needs met by us in our homes, they will look to have their needs met by whoever else is most available. I have so often seen the tragedy of teens who have become involved in lives filled with immoral decisions—even children raised in church life—who are in our basement weeping at their scars. They confess to my older children that their parents know nothing about what has gone on in their lives. Before these times, I read statistics about children with only mild interest.

When the statistics became personal, though, and we saw up close the wounded lives of precious friends, I became more convicted about how vigilant I need to be as a mother. I need to be there protecting, loving, and training my children. I need to be physically available to them in order to talk to them, love them, help them, and bless them.

I believe the Spirit of God is calling mothers to a strategic ministry in a unique time. I know I risk making moms angry at me for saying this, but the stakes in our children's lives and the potential consequences are too high to ignore. God intended that righteousness be passed down from one generation to another through the family. If we don't take personal responsibility to train and disciple our children and to teach them that they are responsible to teach others, then we will risk losing the battle for our children's hearts and minds, and the battle for the next generation will be compromised, perhaps beyond recovery.

One of the greatest works we will ever do is to light the fire in our children's hearts for becoming kingdom workers. I attended a two-week conference in England last summer with Sarah. We spent one week in Oxford and one week at Cambridge, hearing from some of the best Christian leaders and writers in the world. Topics ranged from bioethics to the judicial system to the influence of media on the lives of contemporary children to philosophy. It was very heady stuff.

What especially struck me, though, was how poignantly one issue was presented again and again in every speech and presentation. It seemed that most of these leaders felt this generation of youth seem to be morally, spiritually, and emotionally bankrupt. This was a constant hot topic of concern in many of the talks. Yet no one seemed to have any practical solutions to turn this fact around.

What they clearly presented is that the imagination of this generation has been captivated by television, movies, magazines, computer, and blogs. For the first time in history, their morals are defined by something outside of the direct influence of their families. Yet this influence comes directly into their homes through the constant availability of media. Instead of being influenced by personal relationships in family and church, this generation of children is being shaped and influenced spiritually and morally by what they are taking in from impersonal machines and devices. God designed the home and family to influence children for God, not the media.

It's not all bad, but even if they glean some good elements of truth from media, morals are more personal than just a set of beliefs. A real human being is designed by God for interpersonal interactions that technology can only counterfeit or displace, but never actually replace. Compassion and love are lived out in real, personal relationships. A television or monitor replaces the voice of real people with a false reality projected impersonally onto an impersonal screen. Morality learned from images that are separated from a real human, no matter how "real" they may seem, ultimately will be empty and lifeless because there is no real heart and mind interaction or relationship.

It is not enough only to teach our children all the things they should know. We need to pass on to them a heart that is filled with the love and compassion of God for others. Only when they are acting out God's love for others will they be able to glimpse His own love for them and the world. That is how thankfulness for grace is learned, and how humility grows from an understanding of what it cost Christ to lay down His life for us. That kind of reality is passed on only by a real relationship.

As we walk in the good works that God prepared for us to do (see Ephesians 2:10), we model for our children what kingdom work looks like. We help build into their very beings that they are to be a part of the great work of God in the world—that their personality, skills, mind, and soul have been designed by God to be invested in a cause greater than themselves. When we unlock their potential for service, calling, and ministry, we reveal their innermost design—they were made in the image of God to be purposeful and to invest their lives in a meaningful work which will last throughout eternity.

But before I can pass on that grand vision of life to them, I must first own it myself, and own my stewardship for the world. I must perceive myself to be part of God's work not just in a personal ministry, but in the way I raise my children and help them find their place in God's kingdom. I must see my children as future stewards of God's kingdom work, not just as recipients of knowledge about the kingdom.

Second Key: Personal Responsibility

I must learn to take initiative to do something myself to serve. Each of us has been given gifts by the Holy Spirit of God so that we may serve others in the church and the world. This simply means that God desires for us to use the gifts given to us. It will look different for each woman and for each family, but if we are made in the image of God and walking according to His desires and by His Spirit, then the things that are on God's heart will be on our heart. Redeeming and restoring people back to His love is always on God's heart, and so it should be on ours.

Recently I was talking to a friend on the phone, and she found out I was going to write this chapter.

"I think you should write to these women about how important it is for each of us to take the initiative to reach out to others. We shouldn't just sit by and wring our hands and watch the world go downhill without trying to do something."

I asked my friend what she meant.

"It seems to me that most people wait around for something to happen. Instead of having someone over for lunch, inviting someone to breakfast in their home, or starting their own small prayer group or Bible study in their home, they just wait for someone else to do it. That's why so many people feel isolated and lonely—no one is taking the opportunity to reach out and be a blessing."

This friend is always doing something for someone—a child, an adult, someone ill in the hospital, a neighbor who has lost a loved one. She has been confronted with the death of all her siblings and most of her close relatives. She has only a frail, sick mother left to care for. Yet she has allowed God, in all of these situations, to teach her and show her what her own needs were in sadness, pain, and difficulty. She has then used these lessons to help her know better how to reach the needs of others God brings into her life.

Similarly, when children are brought into a life of helping and serving others, they blossom into the kinds of mature adults whose lives are poured out for others. They don't learn how to serve just by knowing what God says about service. They learn how to serve by breathing in and living out the atmosphere of service we create for them at home.

How do we apply this? I try to take time alone with the Lord at least once a year to specifically pray, "Father, through Your Holy Spirit show Clay and me what work You would have us do as a family this year to further your gospel and to serve other people." Then Clay and I write down a list and begin to consider practical ways in which we will move toward this work He has placed on our hearts.

For myself, I feel strongly that one key focus of my life is to encourage others in their walk with the Lord. I feel God wants me to help others stay committed to His ways. In my planning time, I will write down articles I think He would want me to write. I write down people who need money or support for their mission. I write down specific people who need a card, e-mail, or letter from me in which I communicate love or appreciation for their friendship or life. When I make it practical, I am taking personal responsibility to be an encourager.

Third Key: Training

I have come to see personal training as vital to living this kingdom life. When I was a young Christian, I attended numerous training seminars in which I was instructed how to lead Bible studies, ask relevant questions, and lead prayer in a group of young women. I also learned how to share my personal testimony, and to lead someone to Christ using Scripture. Consequently, because of training in these simple principles, I learned that I, a normal person, could have quite an impact on others. All it required was for me to step out in faith, practice the simple principles of personally and spiritually influencing others, and watch the Lord work in and through my life.

Training gives confidence and effectiveness. When we hosted our conferences, we trained each of our youth how to serve the adults, how to do their jobs at the conference, and how to reach out and encourage others in the name of Christ. With a small amount of training and input, and the opportunity to use their training for others, most of the children who have worked alongside their parents at our conferences have become very mature servant leaders. They know how to help and serve in many other venues the Lord has brought into their lives.

You probably don't have a conference to get your children involved in serving, but you do have a training ground that is no less strategic and effective for shaping your children's hearts for service. Wherever God has placed your family to influence others for Him—home, church, mission, community, neighborhood—is also a God-provided training opportunity for your children. Whenever you are involved in ministry, involve your children with you. There is no more powerful opportunity to influence your children's hearts, motivate them to serve God, and train them for service and ministry than to be with you when you serve and minister to others.

⁰³

These three keys are just a starting point. I have also learned one more principle of ministry that has helped my own children and others grow in their capacity as leaders. It is simply that I serve them personally. If I work my children to exhaustion without helping them to refuel and rest, I am tempting them to feel used and abused. I have seen parents who expect their older children to babysit, cook, serve others, and be joyful, but they don't encourage rest. Too many times I have seen this lead to deep resentment in the child's life.

Jesus, however, showed us a different kind of leadership. He was keenly aware of His disciples' needs even in the midst of ministry. He often fed His disciples and others who were hungry. He would take them by themselves alone—to talk to them, instruct them, and pour out His love on them. Even the night before He died, Jesus was serving His disciples. Away from the crowds in a private room reserved just for their Passover meal, Jesus washed their feet, served them the meal, instructed them, and spoke of His love for them. He treated them as precious to Him, knowing that it would help prepare them to give generously of their own lives when the time came.

Recognizing the needs of my own children to receive encouragement and validation in their personal relationship with me, I have sought to represent the voice of the Lord in their lives. I look for ways to carve out time alone with my children—take them out for a special meal, go up to the mountains for a picnic and hike, or even take them to a special hotel for an overnight getaway. It gives me focused time with them to lavish them with love and affirmation. Our time together is focused on appreciating them for the work they have done, investing personally in their life and dreams, and envisioning how God can use them. When their cups are full, they will have more to give to others out of what is stored up in their hearts. I am careful to monitor their lives so that I can see that they are spiritually, emotionally, and physically refueled for future service.

When we embrace this call to servanthood and ministry, both in our own lives and in the training of our children, we are involved in the advancement of the influence of the kingdom of God on earth. How amazing it is that even if we don't have a title or a degree, we mothers can be a part of preparing an army that will advance the influence of light into this world. We do it simply by being faithful to do God's work in and through our home—that strategic and divinely-designed training ground for heaven's work on earth.

Praying with Faith

DEAREST LORD AND KING ❧ *You are my light and my life. I have no light to give to others than the light that is from You.* ❧ *Open my eyes that I might better see and understand the battle that is raging in our world for the souls of my children. Help me to understand the importance of engaging them in the battle for righteousness, accepting the accountability that comes from choosing to invest their lives along with others who are involved in redeeming back the world to Yourself. Help me to tame my schedule and responsibilities so that I might have opportunities to influence my children moment by moment as they grow into young adults.* ❧ *Teach me how to become more strategic with the moments you have given me, so I can make the most of every opportunity (Ephesians 5:15). Give me glimpses into the souls of my children so I can better understand how to reach their hearts. Give our family eyes of compassion for those around us who have needs we can meet. Build my children into godly leaders amidst the warp and woof of our lives. Will You, the greatest leader of men, lead my children into Your work and ways?* ❧ *For Thine is the kingdom and the power and the glory forever and ever. Amen.*

☙

Walking by Faith

"For we are His workmanship, created in Christ Jesus for good works, which God prepared beforehand so that we would walk in them" (Ephesians 2:10). As you consider your life and the life of your family, what "work" has God given you a heart to do, or especially equipped you to do, that your children can do with you? What passions or compassions are part of your family culture that can be invested in ministry to others?

"But thanks be to God, who always leads us to triumph in Christ, and manifests through us the sweet aroma of the knowledge of Him in every place. For we are a fragrance of Christ to God among those who are being saved and among those who are perishing" (2 Corinthians 2:14-15). Sometimes when our family is just being ourselves–playing together at the park, eating at a restaurant, shopping–others will stop us to say how nice it is to see a family enjoying each other. Other times, though, I have had to train the manners of my children, and their habits of talking to each other, to help them to behave in a loving and civilized way. In what areas do your children need more training and instruction in order to be a "fragrance" of Christ to those God brings into your life? How can you affirm them and help them understand what a testimony even small children can be to bring His light to others?

Jesus looked at the needs of others and, instead of being critical of them had compassion for their "lostness" (Matthew 9:36). Make a list of things you can do with your children to help them own their responsibility to bring His light to the world. For example, you might invite neighbors over to a Christmas open house, find out more about their needs, and pray for them. Or you could sponsor a child overseas through an organization like Compassion International and regularly pray for your new family member.

Walking with
Trust
as a Mother

CHAPTER EIGHT

Finding Grace Every Day to Walk with God

But the fruit of the Spirit is love, joy, peace,
patience, kindness, goodness, faithfulness,
gentleness, self-control; against such things
there is no law. ... If we live by the Spirit, let
us also walk by the Spirit.

GALATIANS 5:22-23,25

After a nonstop weekend of speaking at a parenting conference, my spiritual and emotional tanks were nearly empty, and I was just keeping on by clinging to the thought of a relaxed dinner with our friends and family as soon as the conference was over. I knew our kids were just about as tired after working the book tables and leading the music all Friday and Saturday. They were quite ready for some focused attention from their parents.

It had been a truly blessed weekend. We had seen many parents encouraged and felt that the Holy Spirit had worked in the hearts and minds of the moms and dads who had come. There was a real sense of renewed life and peace as they caught the biblical picture of passing on righteousness from one generation to another through their homes.

But we were now more than ready to get out of our conference "uniforms" and formal shoes, throw on some comfortable clothes, and fall apart together at our friend's home. Some of our board members lived in town, and we all cherished their home as a place of total refuge and freedom where we could be our own interesting selves and spend the evening in a rousing round of shared secrets, laughter, feasting, and dreaming. Good fellowship, comfy couches, and some favorite foods were the perfect way to end the day.

We had also learned from experience that our children's energy would also be winding down by now. When the conferences were over and they had been "just as good as they could be," they also wanted to fall apart. The after-conference evening is always a time of regrouping for our family, when we hear all the tales of the day and generally get a blow-by-blow report from the kids—the fun times, the boring moments, a naughty word that had been shared, a fuss or tangle among the children, and all the other happenings of their time.

Clay and I always valued this time because it was our chance to right all wrongs, sympathize with their plights, correct bad attitudes, and pour on thanks and appreciation for their willingness to work with such patience at the conferences. Often, amid the sharing and complaining and stresses, we knew that what was needed most was a loving caress, a kiss, a tasty meal, and a good night of sleep for our children's exhausted bodies. Yet we did see them growing by leaps and bounds in learning the life of giving and reaching out to others, even at their young ages.

At this conference, however, our reprieve was to be put off for a couple more hours as some of the families asked us to join them for dinner. "We have reserved a private room for our group with a banquet-style table so we can spend some more time picking your brains and asking you questions." Though we love being with friends and colleagues, tonight we were just exhausted and desperate to get home.

We tried to communicate that we so appreciated their invitation, but that our children were quite tired and wondered if we could possibly join them another time.

"Well, you have to eat anyway, so come on and join us!" insisted the enthusiastic host. But then he added, "We really want to ask you more about your philosophy of grace-based discipline and parenting." I really didn't want to know what kinds of questions he had in mind, but it didn't take long to learn that he disagreed with messages he had heard by me, and views that he knew about from Clay's book, *Heartfelt Discipline*. He got right to his point.

"We want to know how you can maintain authority in the eyes of your children without a way to create healthy fear and respect. Your approach to discipline sounds permissive. Don't you believe that the Bible instructs parents to use strict discipline?" I didn't answer his question. He was not really interested in an answer, but obviously wanted to expound his own opinion.

There was no question in my mind about his views. He represented the adversarial view that parents must catch and punish every willful sin and every act of foolishness in a child. To fail to do so or to be inconsistent, in that view, would amount to disobedience of God's commands and the risk of raising an undisciplined and rebellious child.

He smiled and continued. "We just want to get to know you and your children up close, watch how you relate, and try to understand just how this works. So, how can you refuse such a great discussion?"

Yikes! Now I knew our views were being put to the test, and at the worst possible time. Some friends had warned us of the harsh and rigid child-training philosophies that had been promoted in the area. I knew we might encounter them, but it had never occurred to me that we would do so at the very moment that both parents and children were ready to crash and most vulnerable! By God's timely grace, a waiting mom from the group conveniently intervened and gave me an easy exit, so I just let the man's challenge drop.

And yet I knew, in the midst of the crowd of people talking and pursuing Clay at one end of the room, and others talking to me in the foyer, we would soon all sit down to eat together ... and talk. I felt a dread building in my weary heart as I wondered how four-year-old Joy would manage the test put before her, let alone my weary, wiggly little boys. Joy hadn't had a nap in two days, and she had stayed up too late the night before. I felt like a defendant on trial, and to add to the drama I hadn't even had a chance to warn Clay or our children.

As our group poured into the restaurant, I managed to take the kids aside and tell them how very much I would appreciate it if they could employ their self-control just a little longer. I promised all manner of rest and fun when we got home and then went to my seat praying they would manage to keep it together.

By the time I made it back to my chair, three other adults had taken the seats between Joy and me, so that she ended up down the table with a friend instead of in her rightful spot next to me. Because we were a group of around twenty, it took longer than normal to get our food. I made sure that Joy had a roll and butter to appease her during the wait. I also passed down a coloring book with some bright colors.

During the wait for the food, Clay and I proceeded to explain what discipleship looked like at different phases of our children's lives. Clay shared that gentle love and attention should be given in the early years along with moment-by-moment instruction in the ways of life—learning to obey, practicing self-control, relating lovingly to siblings, choosing between right and wrong, and understanding what it meant to be good and godly. I added that meeting the children's needs for love, affection, rest, nutritious food, and lots of time at home in a comfortable, unhurried environment gave a physiological strength to their bodies so that they could respond to the training. Finally, I concluded that verbal and mental stimulation from lots of talking, reading, and playing were also necessary in order to fill our children's emotional, spiritual, and mental cups.

When is that food going to come? This was the longest dinner in history. I knew I was bored and tired of hearing us talk. Weariness was really beginning to set in for me. How long would my children last before one of them burst a gasket? I knew that I was about to explode.

Finally, the food was served. I breathed a sigh of relief, sensing that our grace-based parenting style defense was not falling on receptive hearts. We had poured out our hearts and there was not much more to be said. I was proud of my sweet children, behaving in at least a minimally civilized and content manner as they chatted together at the end of the table. Everyone, adults and children, finally quieted down as we began to munch on our long-awaited food.

Suddenly, in the midst of the quiet, little Joy lifted her high voice with its little lisp and said loudly enough to garner the attention of every parent at that table. "Hey, Mom, look down here. This is fun! If you poke your straw real hard into a French fry, you can pick it up and eat it off of the straw! Look at me!"

At this point, all eyes turned to focus on my quite oblivious little girl. She began forcefully poking her French fries onto a straw, using it to dip them in ketchup then eating them off the end with a flourish. She was quite proud of her accomplishment and enjoying herself immensely.

I went cold and felt that every eye had been swiftly turned on Clay and me to see how we would respond to such obvious immaturity at a banquet table. I immediately felt the pressure to perform well for these parents who, I was sure, expected me to control my child's unacceptable lapse in table manners.

Of course my first impulse with such an audience was to save face and correct my daughter by saying something like, "Joy, you know our family rule about French fries. You may never poke a French fry with a straw!"

The absurdity of such a statement almost made me laugh. At this moment, my dear friend right next to me kicked me under the table to get my attention. With a discreet lean in my direction, she whispered fiercely in my ear, "Don't you dare discipline Joy in front of all these people. She hasn't done anything wrong. She's been as good as gold! She's just being a typical four-year-old. Don't embarrass her or she will resent you and feel hurt!" Lowering my eyes, I think I mumbled something like, "That looks like a lot of fun, Joy. How about trying to finish your dinner and then we can go home and play!" *Please, please, let us go home!*

I hardly remember the rest of the dinner or the reactions of the other parents. I do vividly remember the feeling in my stomach—the pressure I felt when I was under the burden of the implied or imagined standards of people around me that I felt I needed to uphold. It was indeed a burden. Looking back, I have no doubt that the Lord was teaching me a lesson, and I thought about that moment many times after the incident.

☙

I have felt pressure many other times in my life as a mother to live under the expectations and laws of other Christian parents. I was tempted to act harshly in correcting Joy just to show that I understood the rules and to prove that I was in control of my own children. Trying to live up to someone else's arbitrary standards produced a yoke of pressure to perform and guilt for not being a perfect parent.

But I came to the realization that no matter how many rules I make, my children by their very nature will come up with areas of challenge I have never conceived. No list of rules or formulas can possibly cover all the possibilities. There is no comprehensive manual for training a child.

There will always be issues like personality (extravert or introvert), gender, or if the child has issues in his or her life such as attention deficit disorder, obsessive-compulsive disorder, autism, or other such challenges. Children change temperaments sometimes when they are on medications for asthma or other illnesses, they are highly affected by stress (moving to a new home, the death of a grandparent, high expectations, even busyness), and that's not to mention the personality-altering power of teenage hormones! Each and every situation must be evaluated and considered differently, according to Scripture, family values, training, and the children's needs. There is no one-size-fits-all formula, biblical or otherwise.

When we are seeking to discipline and train our children, we are not seeking to train them as morally perfect robots. We have freedom to enjoy a free-flowing relationship with our children, to love them, and and to respond to the need of the moment with wisdom and grace from the Holy Spirit. We are seeking to give them a heart for righteousness and for loving from the very core of their spirits. Reaching our children's hearts requires us to be students of their souls. We want to learn what appeals to them, and understand the things that motivate them, so we can effectively reach their hearts as we train them to love God.

These issues, however, do not apply only to child discipline. They are also relevant to the whole scope of mothering. Each of us mothers has a unique personality, background, experience, and circumstances. The individuality doesn't stop there. We each have our own husband, different numbers and genders of children with unique personalities, different cultural and life experiences, and different financial limitations within which to live. Jesus created families and family culture to be as unique as the animals in His world of creation. We would never compare a giraffe to a penguin and expect them to behave the same. Neither should we expect different families to be the same or live by the same rules. Each family is unique.

I remember reading a book about being a godly woman that a dear friend had recommended. I gleaned some wisdom from several of the chapters, but I found pressure mounting in my heart and tension pounding in my mind as I continued to read this book. The pinnacle of pressure came when the author said that a sign of godliness was if a woman organized the inside of her drawers or not. The implication was that if a woman was orderly in the way she kept the insides of her dresser drawers, then her character would also be in order. To her this was a quality of feminine godliness. What?! Which scripture defines this rule? I have searched he Bible and have yet to find that one.

The reason I felt so overwhelmed is that I knew I would never be able to uphold that author's standard. I spend a lot of time straightening my house and attempting to keep a peaceful, orderly environment that soothes and blesses my family. However, I am a passionate, philosophical, artistic person. I am very relational but love to have time to think, read, write, and drink lots and lots of tea and coffee. It would probably never even dawn on me to use my rare spare time to straighten out the insides of my messy drawers. I would be too busy planning how I was going to change the world, or I would be deep in conversation and counseling with someone. But by that author's extra-biblical standard, I guess I'm doomed to being immature and ungodly!

When Clay and I took a personality indicator early in our marriage after returning home from overseas, the counselor revealed something interesting about my personality that really helped me to understand myself. He said that only about one percent of all Americans would have my personality, and that I was a person who thought outside of the box. He also said that since I was a visionary and idealist, I would probably use my time best exhorting and encouraging people. He told me to expect to think differently about life than most of the people I knew. He also suggested that Clay (a two-percent personality) and I should both seek to work in the areas of ministry that would complement our personalities rather than in situations where we were working in the areas of our weaknesses, or trying to fit ourselves into the expectations of others who did not share our values and visions.

The insights I gained from this personality indicator helped me think differently about myself. It gave me permission to feel okay about what I was like, and what I was motivated to be and do. It also freed me to accept and believe that God has made me good at some things, but not at others. I don't have to excel in everything. That gave me such freedom to know that I had a good place in God's plan just as He had made me.

One of my oldest and dearest friends is gifted at organizing everything. (So is Clay.) She preferred to exert her influence by helping people and by offering hospitality, which we both enjoyed. I, however, preferred to exert my influence in teaching and speaking. We were roommates in Europe and had a delightful partnership in ministry. As we both worked in our areas of strength, we were able to reach more people together because of our complementary strengths. Though she leads Bible studies and disciples others, she would never be as naturally good at doing the things God had gifted me to do. And though I am forced to work at organizing house stuff, events, ministry plans, and so on, I would never be as good at doing all that as my friend. But thank the Lord, I don't have to feel guilty for not being good at everything. God just wants us to be faithful with the gifts He has given us, which I can do. God gave gifts through His Holy Spirit so that the whole body of Christ, each individual member doing their own part, could accomplish His purposes together—the whole is more than the sum of the parts.

This is all true with each of our children, too. God created our children and knows them intimately. We must learn to nurture them in such a way so as to free them up to become the best they can be according to their unique designs. The Holy Spirit alone can give us wisdom to know how to best reach them—this wisdom comes from His Spirit as we seek His Word and pray and glean insight. Even as we are to walk by faith and live by the power of the Spirit in every other area of our lives, we are to walk by faith and live by the power of the Spirit in the area of Christian parenting and in training our children. When we do, we'll be free to be the moms He made us to be.

☙

In our seminars and in letters we receive from people all over the world, there seems to be a common plea: "Just tell me the formula for how to train my children! Show me the rules that will make us a good family. I'm so afraid of doing the wrong things or not doing the right things, and being out of God's will. Just tell me what to do and I'll do it."

In response to these kinds of pleas from believers all over the world, Clay and I have discussed and studied at length how this issue applies to parents. It is the crux of the "New Covenant" that Christ initiated, and that is explained in the New Testament. It is the clash of two ways of relating to and living for God: living by rules and laws (living by formula), and living by the power of the Holy Spirit (living by faith). One way of life is defined and driven by fear, the other by faith and freedom.

These two ways of life are obvious in the life and ministry of Jesus. The Pharisees were the ruling class of religious leaders during the time of Christ. They held to a strict form of religion and attempted to define Scripture with hundreds of very specific and legalistic applications on how to carry out the letter of God's Law. Their lives were entirely justified and given meaning by the works they performed and the laws they kept. They judged themselves and others by how well they were able to carry out the letter of these rules and laws.

Jesus, however, was very harsh with them. He called them "a brood of vipers" (Matthew 12:34), rebuking them for their evil hearts. He condemned them as self-serving hypocrites for piling burdens onto the backs of the people, all the manmade laws that they themselves were unwilling to keep (Matthew 23:2-5). They ruled over the people with laws and formulas that put them in bondage to guilt and shame.

Jesus came to set the people free from that bondage, not by creating a better set of rules, but by offering His grace. He did not come and say, "Blessed are the Law keepers." Rather, He radically proclaimed in His Sermon on the Mount just who the truly "blessed" ones of God are—the poor in spirit, the mourners, the gentle, those who hunger and thirst for righteousness, the merciful, the pure in heart, the peacemakers, and the persecuted" (see Matthew 5:1-12). He said He had come to "fulfill the Law" in order that the burden of guilt imposed by that Law would be satisfied and relieved, and all could find freedom in Him (Matthew 5:17-20). That is the grace He offered. The apostle John would later say, "For the Law was given through Moses; grace and truth were realized through Jesus Christ" (John 1:17).

The Apostle Paul experienced that freedom and grace. As a respected Pharisee himself, he was well-versed in keeping the Law. However, when Jesus invaded his life on the road to Damascus, he discovered a freedom he had never known in the Law. The Law had revealed his sin, but could provide no answer for it, and in fact it only increased the condemnation and guilt he felt before God. It was only the grace he found in Christ that set him free from bondage to the Law (Romans 7:7-25).

Paul eloquently, spiritually, and logically condemns legalism in his powerful epistle to the church in Galatia. He had ministered throughout Galatia in Asia Minor and found many who eagerly responded to and embraced the gospel of Christ. But a group of Jews there was preaching that it wasn't enough just to be a believer in Christ. They argued that the Galatian Christians, both Jews and non-Jews, needed to keep the Law and be circumcised as well in order to show they belonged to God.

Circumcision was an Old Testament ritual and sign that God required for all Jewish men. To these so-called Judaizers, it was a sign of justification. However, Paul rebuked and corrected their false teaching: "[K]nowing that a man is not justified by the works of the Law but through faith in Christ Jesus, even we have believed in Christ Jesus, so that we may be justified by faith in Christ and not by the works of the Law; since by the works of the Law no flesh will be justified" (Galatians 2:16). Jesus' death on the cross set free all those who believed in Him from the condemnation of trying to earn justification by keeping the Law. "[F]or if righteousness comes through the Law, then Christ died needlessly" (2:21). The grace of Jesus was enough.

Paul forcefully asserts to the Judaizers that the liberating and grace-giving Spirit of Christ now lives in every believer. "It was for freedom that Christ set us free; therefore keep standing firm and do not be subject again to a yoke of slavery" (5:1). He makes himself clear: "But I say, walk by the Spirit, and you will not carry out the desire of the flesh. ... But if you are led by the Spirit, you are not under the Law" (5:16, 18). No amount of rule keeping, legalistic standards, or rigid performance can make us good, control our sin, or produce godly character in us or in our children. That will come only by God's grace, through the Holy Spirit creating His fruit in our lives. "If we live by the Spirit, let us also walk by the Spirit" (5:25). We live "by grace through faith" (see Ephesians 2:8-9), not by guilt through laws.

႙

What does all this mean in the everyday moments of my life as a mother? I know I cannot be perfectly righteous, nor can my children perfectly keep all my laws, rules, and ideals. But the very Son of God who is absolutely perfect, the best Child ever born, didn't leave formulas about how to raise godly children. He had something better in mind—He left us His Spirit. He showed me how to build my children into godly disciples of Christ by grace, through faith, in the power of His Holy Spirit. The Spirit leads me into maturity as I walk with God and obey His Word, and it is the same for my children. Maturity is a process, a journey, and it takes time. There simply is no method or formula that can promise parenting success. Instead, our tools are relational and spiritual—grace, faith, patience, love, and the power and fruit of the Holy Spirit.

As I have lived through the many seasons of my children's lives and now have children in their twenties, I wish I had known more about grace when I was a younger parent, for their sakes. There are times when I wonder why God would allow or choose someone like Clay or me to be speakers and writers focused on training parents how to disciple their children. We are not perfect by any means. We make mistakes with our children. Sometimes we lose our tempers or become irritable. Weariness and fatigue has dampened our spirits at times, and it has caused us to be less than regular in having devotions. There have been times when my children have appeared to me more as aliens than as my beloved own—times when I would think, "How could they behave that way" or "How could they think that way" or "Where did that personality quirk come from?" Even worse, there have been times when my feelings were neutral or even negative about one child or another in the midst of a crisis with them. I would think, "How can I call myself a committed Christian mother and have such negative feelings toward one of my own children?"

Yet, one of the most prominent themes of Scripture that has carried me through the "seasons of travail" in my journey of parenting is the concept of living in God's grace, resting in Christ's care, and walking in the power of the Holy Spirit. I have come to understand that I am not responsible to reach my children's hearts, build godly character in their lives, or even get them to behave. The Holy Spirit is responsible.

Of course, we are God's chosen instruments in the lives of our children—to model Christ's character, to teach the truths of Scripture, and to be God's hands and voice. Yet only He can work in their hearts to give them the desire to respond to Him. We make pathways in their brains so that they will be familiar with His ways, but the Holy Spirit artistically conducts a symphony of words and images in the minds, dreams, and consciences of our children to bring them to the throne of God and to cause them to bow their knee.

The same Holy Spirit that teaches my children, helps me learn moment by moment how to love and guide them along their paths of life as they grow into adults. As I spend time each day in the Word and in prayer, God brings His principles to mind and gives me the grace and wisdom I need whatever that day may hold. God gives Clay and me great freedom to live within the confines of our personalities as we seek to be the parents God created us to be.

☙

The passions, dreams, and values on our hearts will create a unique family culture that will become the heritage our children will take with them after they leave our home. The Holy Spirit is the conductor of the unique symphony of the Clarkson household, taking the notes of our lives and ways and turning them into a song that will bring Him glory. Even as there are a vast number of symphonies that are beautiful, though varying in style and design, so each family may play or sing a different song, all within the context of being obedient to live out the will of God together.

Beyond even that, the Holy Spirit fills in the holes that Clay and I have left. I have seen that my children, as they have matured, are rich in their souls, and loving and passionate about the Lord and His kingdom. Yet it happened gradually and in spite of our own imperfections. I think our children knew that we loved and accepted them as whole persons even though they, like us, had lots of immaturity and sin to overcome. They grew best in the freedom they had in an environment of love, grace, and faith.

We can't by sheer force or the right rules or the right devotional curriculum make our children spiritual. We can shape their hearts and minds, and "bring them up in the discipline and instruction of the Lord" (Ephesians 6:4), yet there is still a mysterious process by which the Holy Spirit leads our children to see their need for Christ, and to choose to respond to Him. But that process is entirely led by God's grace, informed by Christ's love, and carried out with the help of the Holy Spirit. We can instruct, and train, and influence, but in the end we must trust God to work in their hearts.

No, we don't have a rule about French fries and straws. We just have committed hearts towards our kids and the desire to shape their souls to respond passionately to their Creator. He came to us with grace and truth to bring life and wholeness into our hearts. We strive to follow His example in the lives of our children. We have left the path of legalism. We walk in the power of the Holy Spirit and rest in His grace.

Praying with Faith

DEAR GRACIOUS FATHER ~ *How thankful I am that You have covered me with Your unconditional love and acceptance. How relieved I am that Christ has freed me not only from the burden of sin, but from the burden of living under the rule of law, whether real or imagined. How grateful I am for the ministry of the Holy Spirit in my life, leading me into your grace. ~ Help me to dwell in the freedom I have as Your child to rest in Your grace, even amid my own immaturity and failures. Help me to live in the knowledge that You are ever cheering me on and supporting me in my journey toward Your beautiful character. May it become more evident in my life every day. Help me to extend that sweet grace and love to my children so that they may perceive the life-giving love You have for them by learning it from me. ~ Because of Jesus' grace I come to you. Amen.*

അ

Walking by Faith

Galatians 5:1 tells us that, "It was for freedom that Christ set us free; therefore keep standing firm and do not be subject again to a yoke of slavery." Are there any ways in your life as a mom that you are trying to live up to the false expectations of others? Has that ever felt as though you were bearing a yoke of slavery, as this verse suggests? In what ways does God want you to release any areas of bondage so you may live in His freedom? How do you need to extend that freedom to your children?

List the areas of immaturity in your children that bother you the most. How are you extending God's grace and love to them in these areas? How do they respond when you show them grace? How can you better encourage them and communicate your acceptance of them just as they are? Tell each of your children something that you appreciate about them today.

Peter tells us that "love covers a multitude of sins" (1 Peter 4:8). In what way does that verse apply to the relationships in your life with those who have fallen short of your standards? How does God's love "cover a multitude" of your own sins? As we learn to become more like Jesus in our role as mothers, wives, and friends, how can we use this verse to give more grace to others through our attitudes and in our actions?

CHAPTER NINE

Living Confidently as a New Creation of Christ

Just as a father has compassion on his
children, so the LORD has compassion on
those who fear Him. For He Himself knows
our frame; He is mindful that we are but
dust.

PSALM 103:13-14

March promised to be an adventurous month.

Over a year before, we had accepted an invitation to speak in Australia and New Zealand. It would be a wild ride indeed, but it also sounded like a grand adventure. Going "Down Under" would be an exotic experience—dreams of kangaroos, koala bears, and outback exploration had captured our imaginations. But no more so than the captivating idea of seeing the land where *The Lord of the Rings*, one of our family's favorite movie series, had been filmed.

At two weeks out, we were getting pretty excited. I felt I had my talks together, which was a relief. After all, parenting and motherhood were my most comfortable topics so I felt confident about my messages. Although I would be speaking at a comfort-challenging pace of twenty-nine times in eighteen days in five cities, I was able to put aside the talks and use the last two weeks for packing for the trip and providing for the boys staying at home. Plans had changed in the last months so this became the first big trip with just the girls. The boys had classes and work schedules they simply could not skip, so Clay had volunteered to man the home front.

On the rare occasions that I leave the boys, I always like to fill the freezer with homemade food and leave the house in tip-top shape so that they feel amply provided for while I am gone. My mothering ideals dictate a high standard of nurture for the boys and Clay, and I wanted to leave them fully supplied, even though we would be gone for only a short time. It was especially important because I felt somehow that I would feel better speaking about the ideals of motherhood to this new group if I left everyone back home in peace and with plenty of provision.

That was what I was thinking one very cold morning just before our trip as I got up early to go grocery shopping. The weather in Colorado in the spring is often extremely unpredictable, and this morning was no exception. A cold snap had come over the mountains, sending the temperature plummeting, That morning the thermometer read five below zero. We were used to managing the roads in snowy weather, but we were not used to such unusually frigid temperatures.

As I turned on the car to warm it up, I glanced up through the fog of my breath and was shocked. The inside of the car seemed to have grown a million freckles during the night. Brown spots, large and small, were splashed and spattered over every inch of the interior: seats, dashboard, ceiling, doors, windows, and carpet. After several seconds of letting the shock settle in, I finally began looking around to find what could have caused this incredible phenomenon.

Then I spotted the empty soft drink can. Someone had left a full, unopened can in the car the night before. In the frigid weather it had frozen and exploded, and now dark spots were scattered across every square inch of that poor car's interior. I simply couldn't deal with it then since I had several appointments that morning. I would have to find out who left the drink in the car later and have them clean it up.

I should have known right then that I was in for it. The surprising discovery in my car began a crazy next few weeks. My exciting March started early and proved to be quite an adventure all right, though not the one I had planned. It continued the next day after a busy morning at church. We hadn't even ridden in the still-not-yet-cleaned car. When we were all just settling in for an hour of relaxation with the paper and some hot chocolate, I went upstairs to change clothes.

As I entered the bathroom connected to our bedroom, my foot encountered something it was not expecting: a puddle of water. Looking down, I yelled for Clay as I ran into the closet and realized that my entire bathroom, walk-in closet, and half of my bedroom was absolutely sopping wet with pooling water. Rushing up the stairs and squishing through the marshy carpet, Clay managed to shut off the water flow under our sink and then ran down to the garage below where we found it flooded in real earnest. The cold weather had burst our pipe, as well as the soft drink can, which sent water spewing all over the furniture, books, and pictures stored in our garage.

We forgot our quiet Sunday afternoon in a sudden rush of ripping up carpet, moving all the furniture out of our bedroom and the garage, and employing every available towel in the house to sop up the mess. I watched as the kids helped pile all of my stuff out in the hall, wondering if I would ever see it all again. My clothes, books, and papers somehow made it to every corner of the house in the next few days since we had to live and sleep in other rooms while we waited for the carpet to dry and the rental company to fix the extensive damage.

And that just began the countdown of adventurous days before our trip. The ensuing weeks were a comedy (calamity?) of errors. We ate fast food almost every meal (I could only stand so many messes at once), I missed a piano lesson out of sheer forgetfulness and had to pay for it anyway, and I found an entire stack of overdue library books. (There are times when I think the Clarkson family partially funds the local library.)

One late evening I had a ridiculous, heated argument with one of my teen boys about the inappropriateness of contemporary clothing. I know so much better than to engage in an argument like this, especially when the subject is abstract and not specifically relevant to the child at that moment. But I felt so much like arguing with someone, so much like being outraged against something, that I jumped in with abandon. Quite mature, don't you think?

The next day, I managed to get my credit card stuck in a gas pump slot because I absentmindedly stuck it into the receipt feeder instead of the card reader. It took ingenuity, broken fingernails, and finally a screwdriver to pry the silly thing out. Wouldn't you think that after filling up my car countless times at the same gas station with the same machines, I would know to put my card in the credit card slot instead of the receipt slot? Not to mention the fact that I had to really push it to get it in there in the first place. Shouldn't I have suspected that I had it in the wrong place? (Explaining this to Clay was rather interesting.)

By the time our departure date rolled around, I had barely managed to stuff my last necessaries into my suitcase, let alone make two weeks' worth of tasty, homemade meals for my boys. It seemed that the only gift I was leaving was a pile of clothes stacked up in the laundry room. I knew how thoughtful Clay would consider this gift. As I got into the front seat of our van with him, he suddenly noticed our car's speckled appearance. "What in the world happened in here?" he asked. "What are all these spots all over the dashboard and seats?"

Whoops. Guess I forgot about that mess.

I sighed and tried not to notice those brown spots on the hour-long drive to the airport. When we had finally checked our bags and buckled ourselves into the flight to Auckland via LA, I took a deep breath. It felt like the first time I had sat down in the last two weeks. However, as the reality of the trip hit me, I couldn't really relax because of how inadequate I suddenly felt.

After the last few days, how could I possibly speak to all those moms about the ideals of biblical motherhood? After all, Clay and I have a ministry about training parents to build godly character into the lives of their children, I write books on motherhood, and I have been in full-time ministry for more than thirty years. Shouldn't I have my act together by now? I felt like writhing in my seat and rolling my eyes at the mess of the past days. The thought of trying to inspire mothers with that picture of failure in my mind began to darken my spirit. The "Phantom Mother" of unrealistic expectations was playing havoc with my conscience. I felt I had been an incompetent wife and mother over the last two weeks.

But as we settled back into our seats and the plane engines began to hum, I decided to have a short time with the Lord to try to calm my anxious mind and heart. I couldn't imagine what could make me feel okay about the last few days, but I had to begin trying to get myself back together. I opened my Bible and just looked down on God's words. There, in black and white on the page before me, came my comfort:

> Just as a father has compassion on his children, so the LORD has compassion on those who fear Him. For He himself knows our frame; *He is mindful that we are but dust.* (Psalm 103:13-14, emphasis added)

I took another deep breath. I closed my eyes. I exhaled. Ah, I sorely needed that. It seemed that God wasn't surprised at my mishaps after all. I don't generally expect much of dust, and neither, it seems, does He. He is a Father who doesn't look for perfection, but for the right heart, even amidst exploding soft drink cans, floods, and credit card mishaps.

০৪

If there is one area almost all mothers I have ever talked to complain about, it is how inadequate they feel to fulfill their roles as good mothers. Feelings of guilt, depression, and inadequacy plague women everywhere I travel. There are so many standards they feel they must live up to.

We have magazines (Christian and secular), television shows, and advertisements, all of which give us the impression that we are supposed to be superhuman wonder moms. Our teeth should be white (not British tea-stained like mine), our bodies tight and sleek, our clothes ever trendy and hip. Our house must be straight, organized, and decorated as perfectly as a Pottery Barn catalog home. Nutritious, homemade meals should be an every night affair. Reading to our intellectual children should be a daily habit after we have hosted stimulating family devotionals.

Our children should have strong character and perfect manners, be able to do the chores of a grown person, and score well on their SAT exams. Being social geniuses, our children should have an acceptable amount of meaningful activities outside the home that will provide them with excellent skills and social poise, while still maintaining that perfect amount of time at home to build loving relationships with their siblings and with us, thus maintaining an atmosphere of complete peace and beauty. The ideals are endless.

Now, ideals in and of themselves are not bad. Being quite an idealist myself, I am continually refining mine for my family and striving hard to accomplish them each year. Ideals keep us moving forward–they give us a goal to aim at. Any woman who doesn't have ideals or plans for her home will quickly be pressured to capitulate to cultural standards and very possibly lose the heart of her children to contemporary culture.

Yet a woman will eventually sink deep into depression or be forced to lower her standards and give up her ideals unless she finds a way to cope with pressure. After all, motherhood is a 24/7/365 job, and relentless in physical, emotional, and spiritual demands for years on end with nary a break. Our children insist on living with us on a daily basis, all the while eating and wearing clothes, making messes, and arguing with each other. Add to that the fact that our culture doesn't validate or affirm the importance of the work we do as mothers, and you have a recipe for discouragement and depression.

I have struggled with depression and inadequacy many times and have often found it hard to know how to cope amid all the pressures and demands of my mothering life. But through the years I have found a place of rest and freedom in my relationship with the Lord, which has made all the difference and helped me to keep going through it all.

I think I first began to learn how to cope when I learned to accept my own imperfections and limitations, choosing instead to live in the reality of God's endless provision of life and grace for me. I came to this point by understanding the security and stability of my relationship in Christ. When the foundation of my own self-image and well-being is established on His love, commitment, and care for me personally (despite floods, depression, dirty cars, and fussy kids), I find the security, peace, and love I need to keep going.

However, a part of living in this place of stability also means that I have to live within the reality of my own limitations. I am imperfect, and no matter how hard I try my children will never be perfect. But when I am resting in the life I have in Christ, my children, in spite of me, still have the opportunity to turn out okay. God is their true source of life, just as He is my source of life, and I am just a tool in His hands that He uses to communicate His life to them. In the end, He is in charge of their souls' destinies, and I have learned to live freely in this knowledge. It has helped to relieve the tension created by trying to balance ideals and reality, and to allow me to enjoy His constant love and help.

It has also helped to remember that I am a frail human being still on the road to maturity. No matter how high I set my standards or how hard I try, I will always make mistakes. Not only that, in a fallen world, with all sorts of possibilities of illness, accidents, bad advice, and the endless presence of a world full of other sinful and immature people, I am bound to find unexpected challenges that thwart my attempts to be competent in my ideals.

But God, as a good Father, has compassion on us, His children, because He is mindful that we are but dust and we live in a dusty world. In other words, He knows we are frail and in need of His compassion in the midst of all of our failures and successes. For me to live in guilt and condemnation because I am immature is not productive. Making choices that will build me into a mature mom who shows more and more of the character of Christ is my constant focus, but it is a long process that does not happen overnight. In the same way that we allow our children many years to mature and to learn to be strong morally, spiritually, emotionally, and mentally, so our heavenly Father is patient with us as we grow.

Part of becoming a mature Christian is learning to die to my old sinful self; not just to sin, but also to my condemnation of myself. My human capacity to fail will always be a disappointment to me. What I have to do is understand and accept my new self, the self who stands forgiven and eternally loved before the throne of my heavenly Father because of what Jesus has done for me. No matter what I do, Jesus is now my Advocate before the Father. God knows and understands that I am a human in need of His grace. But I also need to understand that He sees me as righteous—cleansed from sin, whole, and acceptable—because of what was accomplished on the cross. He sees who I am now in Jesus, not who I see in my mirror. I am a new creation in Christ.

෪

When Sarah was a little girl, she went through a season of life in which she was mesmerized with butterflies. She assembled an amazing collection of specimens that was truly beautiful. There were species of every size and color—huge swallowtails and little blue butterflies, moths with dull brown upper wings that hid a gorgeous underside, and every kind of small butterfly to be found in our Texas fields.

As we pursued this interest through a variety of books and nature stories, I was captivated by the story of the butterfly. Every butterfly begins as a lowly caterpillar inching its way across the ground until it enters the shelter of its cocoon. Once inside, the old miracle happens again. In the darkness of a silken egg, the caterpillar is transformed into a creature that is almost otherworldly in its beauty—a fragile, lovely butterfly. This new creation that was once a simple, earthbound caterpillar is now released from its bonds to soar above the earth, uninhibited and free.

This is such a poignant picture to me of the transformation that takes place in our own lives. When we were once simply creatures who had the burden of sin and condemnation to drag around, Jesus came and transformed us into beautiful new creatures who can now fly freely through life in the power of His resurrection, lifted up by His life and love bestowed on us through the Holy Spirit. Entering the cocoon as a sinful human being in need of transformation is an accurate picture of me apart from Christ, without His grace. Entering the cocoon is a picture of me dying to myself and my limitations. The newly emerged butterfly, beautiful and strong, is a picture of me as I live my life in the love of Christ.

This is such a meaningful picture to me of resurrection life that Clay gave me a gold necklace with a delicate butterfly charm that I wear every day. It reminds me of my new life and the freedom I have to soar in God's presence. It always brings a verse to my mind that I especially love: "Therefore, if anyone is in Christ, he is a new creature; the old things passed away; behold, new things have come" (2 Corinthians 5:17).

I am a butterfly—made new in Him and free to fly.

The Apostle Paul's explanation of what Christ has done for me also helps me understand my new relationship with Him. It helps me understand that I am to walk as a new person:

> Therefore we have been buried with Him through baptism into death, so that as Christ was raised from the dead through the glory of the Father, so we too might walk in newness of life. For if we have become united with Him in the likeness of His death, certainly we shall also be in the likeness of His resurrection, knowing this, that our old self was crucified with Him, in order that our body of sin might be done away with, so that we would no longer be slaves to sin; for he who has died is freed from sin. (Romans 6:4-7)

What does this mean to us as mothers? It means for me that no matter how often I fail, or how weak I am, I can choose to live by faith in Christ's unconditional love. Again, this is a "walking" verse, which means that it is to be chosen daily and gone back to again and again. Christ covered all of my sins—past, present, and future—with His death, and He wants me to live in the power of His resurrection as a new creature, redeemed and forgiven. My part is to choose to believe what He has already offered to me by grace on a moment-by-moment basis.

Paul will go on in his letter to remind us, "Therefore there is now no condemnation for those who are in Christ Jesus" (Romans 8:1). This means that whatever sins you or I have committed in the past, and whatever we might commit in the future, there is no condemnation for us whatsoever because Christ has already paid the penalty. This is the means by which I am able to stay in sweet fellowship with the Lord.

When I lose sight of this fellowship with Christ, and with His complete acceptance of me by grace alone, I can begin to feel discouraged, especially when I compare myself to friends. When I strive to find validation in the wrong ways, I begin to feel inadequate. When I try to find my affirmation from friends, or from my family, or from others at church, I can feel like I'm beginning to live like a caterpillar again, crawling along the ground feeling unbeautiful and unable to fly.

I see the skills and gifts of others and am tempted to feel that I am not doing enough. I see the things that others who are wealthier than

Clay and me can provide for their children and am tempted to think we have not provided for our children well enough. I see others who have lots of loving family, friends, and support systems that build stability into the lives of their children. It tempts me to reflect on how little support or encouragement we have received from family over the years, and makes me sad that my children have had no grandfather and have never known what it was like to have holidays celebrated in the context of a loving extended family. There are endless ways that I can compare myself to others and come up short.

Yet when I consider that God gave Clay and me our children, uniquely designed from our love for each other and for Him, I have to understand that He has provided all that I need to care for their needs. I am not inadequate. I have been given everything needed to raise my children to become the people God created them to be. I have even seen that some of what was lacking in our own family's lives—what we hoped we would give them but could not—has helped my children to be strong in ways they would never otherwise have been. The Holy Spirit has used all of our moves and lack of outside relationships to bond each of our children to each other and us in ways they could not have experienced if others had met all their needs. Each family has its own unique story to tell, with its own particular gifts, opportunities, and history. If you choose to see it that way, it will be a gift to your children based on God's special plans and design for them.

I have also realized that my children hate it when I feel inadequate. They want me to be content and happy in the midst of our own family. When I am accepting the limitations of my life and learning to dance through each day because of the joy I have from being accepted by God, my attitude helps to fill up their cups and make them feel that they are a part of a happy home. As I learn to walk as a new creation who is loved and forgiven, it sets a tone of love and joy in my home that feeds their own hearts with life and love. Depression and disappointment kill life; they are fatal to hope and joy. So I practice making choices every day that help me to live more in the reality of my true life in Christ.

Even with all this assurance of grace, there are times when I do get off course and really blow it. But God always provides instruction even in this. John, the disciple whom Jesus especially loved, deals with the reality of sin. He tells a group of young believers: "If we say that we have no sin, we are deceiving ourselves and the truth is not in us. If we confess our sins, He is faithful and righteous to forgive us our sins and to cleanse us from all unrighteousness" (1 John 1:8-9).

In other words, when we blow it and feel separated from God, we go to Him in prayer. We agree with God that we have fallen short of His will for our lives. We tell Him of our sin and struggle. We then ask Him to forgive us. As in any healthy relationship, honesty, humility, love, and forgiveness have to be a normal part of life. Suppressing, ignoring, or pretending away conflict, immaturity, or sin in our lives gives our children the wrong impression about life.

Your children don't want perfect parents, because they know *they* can't be perfect children. Your children want to know that when their parents sin or act immaturely, they will admit to it, humble themselves before God, and deal with it in a mature way. This gives a healthy pattern to the children as to how they can take care of their own sin and rebellion.

If we try to hide our sin and inadequacy and run away from God amid our struggles, the result is feeling that He is far away from us. When we ignore anyone, we distance and separate ourselves from them, and it is just so with God. The truth is, He is never far away. He desires to be close to us and to walk in intimate friendship with us every day. But in order for this to happen, we must walk with open hearts and hands, coming to Him with our inadequacies and allowing Him to fill in the holes. He will then provide the forgiveness, love, and strength that we need to make it. Other people will eventually fail us because they will never give us the support we so need to keep going on this journey of motherhood. But the Lord never fails, and He is always ready to forgive us, soothe our ruffled souls, and quiet our hearts with His comfort.

಄

The last big understanding to which I've come in my walk with Christ is the knowledge that there is someone out there who really doesn't want me to walk well. Satan would absolutely love for me to stumble and fall or to walk in defeat. It is a pleasure to him when I am caught in guilt and fear, and he is active in trying to bring this about in my life. John, in his Revelation, calls Satan the "serpent," the "dragon," and the "deceiver of the world" (12:9). But the one who "accuses" believers is also the one who has been defeated by Jesus and by faith:

> [F]or the accuser of our brethren has been thrown down, he who accuses them before our God day and night. And they overcame him because of the blood of the Lamb and because of the word of their testimony ..." (Revelation 12:10-11)

Satan would love for us to be discouraged in our journey of motherhood, especially since our work is to build a heart of godliness into our children, shape them into mature disciples of Christ, and send them into the next generation as a heritage of faith. When you are oppressed with constant thoughts of your inadequacy, recognize the voice of accusation for who it is. It certainly isn't God.

God is not surprised that we are weak and sinful—that is why He had to die for us. He is delighted, however, when we take our calling to motherhood seriously. Not only does He give constant grace and zero condemnation, He also becomes our great Encourager, drowning out the discouraging voice of Satan, the accuser of the brethren. Paul makes clear that Jesus is our defender before God, interceding for us:

> What then shall we say to these things? If God is for us, who is against us? He who did not spare His own Son, but delivered Him over for us all, how will He not also with Him freely give us all things? Who will bring a charge against God's elect? God is the one who justifies; who is the one who condemns? Christ Jesus is He who died, yes, rather who was raised, who is at the right hand of God, who also intercedes for us. (Romans 8:31b-34)

Still, I must do my part to seek to live in His grace, rejecting all thoughts that condemn me or discourage me in the task He has given me to do. Even in this way, as I walk as the new, forgiven creature that I am in Christ each day, I am providing a model for my children. It is a picture to which I hope they will return the rest of their lives.

It is literally life changing to walk in the grace of God and to live in the reality of no condemnation—God is not angry at me. It will change you and the way you live. It will change the entire dynamic of your home and family. It will change your legacy and your heritage. There is so much freedom in a family where people are free to fail. When love, forgiveness, and joy are the standards, children are drawn to live joyfully in the presence of the God we so love. They are able to learn about that forgiving, infinite source of renewing love because they see it at work in our lives.

We must learn to walk freely in Christ. This is central to godly motherhood. We must learn to reject doubt and embrace God's renewing, redeeming love for us. We must choose to walk as new creations.

Only in this way will our children be freed to soar as the new creations in Christ they were meant to be. It is as we live in this precious freedom and grace that they will truly see the redemption of Jesus. How blessed we are to know His constant renewing love.

Praying with Faith

DEAR LOVING FATHER ᾧ *Thank You for reminding me that You are "slow to anger and abounding in lovingkindness" (Nehemiah 9:17). I need Your compassion in my life because no matter how hard I try, I fall short of even my own standards of what I think a godly mother should be. I don't have all the answers. I am not always spiritual. Sometimes I don't feel like trying. But You love me and accept me just the way I am.* ᾧ *Lead me away from depression and dark thoughts about my life and my role as a mother. Help me to remember that there is no condemnation for those who are in Christ Jesus (Romans 8:1). Let me bask in Your everlasting love so that I may bring joy and light to my children.* ᾧ *Teach me how to begin every day anew—forgetting the past failures that lie behind, and reaching forward to what lies ahead. Help me to become more mature, loving, and self-controlled for the sake of my children. Let me be a source of your joy in their lives.* ᾧ *Thank You for the constant support and strength you give to me in this journey of motherhood. I appreciate You and am grateful for Your love toward me.* ᾧ *In Jesus' name, as a new creation in Him, I come. Amen.*

 G3

Walking by Faith

In Romans 8:1 Paul declares, "Therefore there is now no condemnation for those who are in Christ Jesus." What things should you allow yourself to feel guilty and inadequate about before God, according to this verse? Take time to list out all the things that make you feel inadequate and write them in a journal or on a piece of paper and then give them to God. Accept His forgiveness and mercy and walk in the newness of your life in Christ.

The Word tells us that God has compassion on those who fear Him. Psalm 103:13-14 reminds us that, "He Himself knows our frame [and] He is mindful that we are but dust." What does this tell you about His understanding of your frailties? It is Satan, the accuser, who would want us to feel discouraged and tempted to quit our ideals; it is God, the encourager, who is willing to love us, help us, and support us through the journey. Whose voice are you going to pay attention to today?

What patterns of thoughts, if any, do you need to change so that you can better experience God's love and affirmation in your life? What must you do to help rid yourself of those thoughts that are soul-killing? Determine to rest in the love and affirmation of the Lord today and resist any thoughts that would discourage you.

Walking with *Heart* as a Mother

— CHAPTER TEN —

Letting God's Truth Fuel the Fires of Motivation

For Your lovingkindness is before my eyes,

and I have walked in Your truth.

PSALM 26:3

Winter had doomed us to live indoors. Sarah was almost three and itching to simply run and shout, and with Joel barely sleeping more than two hours at a time, I felt that I wanted to run outside and maybe do some shouting too. But the frigid temperatures of a European winter effectively locked us into the confines of our tiny Vienna home.

Living in beautiful Wien, as it is called in German, had always been an adventure, but somehow it seemed easier, or more exciting, a few years back when I lived there on my own as a single woman. Now, as a young mom with two toddlers under three years of age, Austria seemed more like a foreign country than ever before, especially in the winter.

Living in a small cottage of about nine hundred square feet made us feel caged as the cold and dreary days marched on and on. Our old, red-tiled house had some old-fashioned charm to it, but that charm meant a leaky roof that sent water dripping down our bedroom walls when it rained and rooms that were perpetually cold. On occasion, a pigeon would find its way into our house through a hole in our attic, flapping its wings and squawking as we tried to catch it. "Walter Pigeon," as we named it, was a delight for Sarah, but not especially thrilling to me. We also shared this tiny place with a young college friend who had come to live with us for six months. For much of her time with us she had been in depression, and such a small house just didn't seem like enough space to contain restlessness and depression all at once.

Clay was serving as an associate pastor in an English-speaking international chapel that was going through a necessary but difficult transition. Some of the relationships among staff and elders were strained, so there were conflicts to confront and drama to endure. He was also helping to draft a new constitution and bylaws which required him to be in his office for long hours. All of this meant I spent much of my time alone. My strolls along the Vienna cobblestones with a leisurely hour for coffee were replaced by monotonous hours in our little house with precious but very whiny little ones always fussing from an ear infection or chest cold.

This was another interesting point in my life as I felt my stress levels dramatically increase with every visit I paid to the Austrian pediatricians. With inadequate German, especially regarding medical terms, I couldn't seem to get to the bottom of my children's constant stream of illnesses. The doctors thought perhaps if they talked louder and more pointedly to me, I would understand their comments. Their loudness of voice and impatience of manner only made me feel more insecure and less able to cope with my sweet babies.

Finally one evening, after a long day of pediatricians, early darkness (the light went so early in winter), restless children, and depressed friends, I felt the world closing in on me. When I told Clay this, he suggested that a trip home to visit my parents might be just what I needed. The mere mention of the thought excited me. To think of having some help, getting some rest, and being loved and spoiled for a few days at home by my own mom—well, that was a prospect to brighten my outlook. Not to mention the fact that everyone there would actually speak English. I couldn't wait to call home.

Waiting late into the night by Austrian time so I could catch my parents in the States in mid-afternoon, I finally called when I knew they would be home. Relaying my saga with much drama, I ended by saying that Clay had suggested that a couple of weeks with them would be just what I needed for refreshment. Dead silence met my enthusiastic announcement. After a short pause, my mom, my best friend and comforter spoke. "Sally, honey, I am so sorry, but you can't come home. Your grandmother died today, and yesterday I found out that Daddy has prostate cancer. I can't deal with any more right now. You will just have to stay there and find a way of coping."

I couldn't believe my ears. Not only could I not go home and forget my worries, it seemed I needed to gird my loins to take up a few more worries as well. As I hung up the phone I felt incredibly isolated and so distant from my home and loved ones in America. I went to bed and wept myself to sleep as brokenheartedly as one of my babies.

Nothing had changed in my restless sleep, but I awakened the next morning knowing a change was needed. I could not sustain the darkness I felt in my spirit. I decided I needed to pull myself together and try to find some light. I asked a friend to stay with the kids for a couple hours so I could get out of the house and spend some time alone.

I bundled up in my full-length coat, wrapped a thick wool scarf around my neck, and pulled on my heavy boots. I knew that I would have quite a hike, making my way through the three-foot snow piled up against our house. I took my Bible and a journal and made my way down our winding, cobblestone street. My destination was a little local konditorei (café) where I could sip cups of coffee for as long as I pleased and ponder just how it was that I was going to make it another day.

The candlelight on the tiny round tables flickered as I walked in the door. A waft of warm air seemed to welcome me into the little sanctuary where I hoped to meet with the Lord. The aroma of coffee mingled with sweet, cinnamon-strewn apple strudel, and I placed an order for both of those treats. The atmosphere was already working on me, and I decided to sit back in my chair and enjoy the sweet respite of this adult moment.

But as I began to rest in the stillness of the moment, I found that my surface feelings wouldn't allow me peace. Before I could actually relax, I was going to have to work through all the worry and struggle mulling around in my soul. It wasn't just the past few days that were causing it; our last two years overseas had been a constant turmoil of work and adventure and very much struggle.

When we had first moved back as a couple to beautiful, old-world Vienna, we had nurtured dreams of bringing the love of Christ to internationals through our ministry in our home and at the international chapel that was in the heart of the city. After Clay graduated from seminary, we had decided that this would be a worthy ministry in which to invest our lives. So we sold and gave away many of our possessions, packed a shipping container, and moved overseas.

Amid our pictures of ministry and hospitality, we also painted rosy visions of our children being surrounded by a variety of leaders, internationals, and diplomats from various countries. There would be great opportunities for them to be exposed to the wideness of the world in such a place. We often pondered the impact such a move would have on our children as we worked hard to raise support, said goodbye to our loved ones, and plunged into our "call" with our whole heart.

There were, of course, many wonderful things about being in Vienna, but those rose-colored glasses had fallen from our eyes very quickly. The last two years had been filled with constant stress and difficulty as we moved twice within the city and struggled to establish ministry and contacts. I had fought through a very difficult pregnancy in a foreign country and had felt the lack of immediate support systems even more acutely because of this.

As I sat in the soft contours of the chair that morning, I found a sense of indignation bubbling up in my soul. *Lord, how can You treat us this way? We gave up everything to come here to follow You. How can I know that You love me if You don't even provide for my basic needs as I'm following Your call? Do You know how lonely I am? Couldn't You at least provide a few friends? If You really loved me, You would provide me what I want, what I need. Is it such an incredible demand to ask for Joel to sleep through the night? A little rest is all I'm asking for, Lord, even a teensy bit of affirmation.*

I glanced heavenward and sighed as I thought all this, and then slowly, almost reluctantly, I opened my Bible and whispered a prayer for help. I found myself turning to Genesis 3, the passage in which Satan tempted Eve. As I read and reread the passage, I asked myself the question, "How did Satan tempt Eve?"

I suppose I felt that somehow this must apply to me, because at that moment I felt very tempted to do something desperate or disobedient. I wasn't sure what, but I felt the desperation of anxiety. But as I read I observed that the first recorded temptation in Scripture came as a result of Satan trying to cast doubt upon the character of God. His temptation to Eve was to make her doubt God's goodness and the rightness of what God had wrought in her life. Satan caused her to doubt God's instruction. He caused her to doubt His provision. He even (and probably most importantly) caused her to doubt God's goodness by suggesting that God had been trying to withhold power and knowledge from Adam and Eve when He commanded them concerning that one tree. Satan deceived Eve into thinking that God was withholding true goodness from her, and that He would not provide what was necessary to satisfy her needs and desires.

Oh, how quickly conviction comes when you open the Word with an open heart. God will use it to change you, just as He did me that day in my Vienna café. I closed my Bible knowing that I, like Eve, was being tempted to doubt God's love for me and to question His goodness in my life. That was the root of my worry, the cause of my despair. Because of all the hard things in my life, I was letting doubt displace my faith, and believing the lie that God would not meet my needs.

But in that coffee shop moment, I knew that the issues of my life were between me and God. I knew I had a choice to make. On the one hand were my overwhelming feelings of loneliness, exhaustion, and discouragement. Because I felt these so strongly, my heart wanted to doubt and to allow bitterness to take over my thoughts and faith. On the other hand, though, was everything I knew from all my years of studying my Bible. All the scriptures I had read and "treasured in my heart" (Psalm 119:11) were there to recall. I knew that God is:

Abounding in lovingkindness. (Psalm 103:8)
With [me] always. (Matthew 28:20)
The One who holds [my] hand when I fall. (Psalm 37:24)
My Shepherd. (Psalm 23:1)

As I pondered and prayed, more verses poured into my brain that declared God's goodness and faithfulness to me as His child and follower. I had to choose now which I would believe: the lies of Satan as he tempted me to look at my struggling circumstances and doubt, or the eternal, life-changing truths of God's overwhelming love and entirely trustworthy goodness to me as His child.

I thought about my own little children. Often, when Sarah wanted to stay up late or when she wanted more candy, I would say no because I didn't think it would be best for her. Because of her immaturity, she would frequently cry and become greatly distressed at my supposed cruelty. She was too young to know what was best for her, and too little to realize that sometimes I must deny things that would harm her.

Similarly, I realized that the essence of my whole walk with God was about me choosing to believe in His goodness the way my little girl believes (usually) in mine, trusting His wisdom and provision for me even if my feelings told me otherwise. I understood anew that walking in the truth meant not just knowing the truth of Scripture, but choosing to actively believe that what Scripture told me was true. It was a decision of my will, not of my own understanding.

Walking in truth, for me, meant planting a flag and choosing to live from that point on within the confines of trust in God's good will for my life. Even in the difficult times, I would choose to wait on Him and submit to His will for my life, trusting what He said in His Word about His faithfulness, love, and care for those who walk with Him.

ଔ

Since that day in that Austrian coffee shop, trusting in God has become a constant theme in my life. I have studied much what it means to live this trust out, and two particular verses in the Psalms have been especially important in helping me learn how to actively and energetically walk in truth.

The first verse is about my focus: "For your lovingkindness is before my eyes, and I have walked in Your truth" (Psalm 26:3).

As I read this psalm, I realized how important it is to keep God's lovingkindness literally "before my eyes." In order to walk in God's truth,

I need to keep His promises and the stories of His goodness constantly in the meditations of my heart. As I choose to remember that God deeply loves me and that He always works for my good, I can be at rest even in the darkness of my present circumstances. Because the reality of His goodness is foremost in my heart, I can trust that He is actually in the darkness with me, whether or not I can see Him or feel His presence.

The second verse is about my direction: "Teach me Your way, O LORD; I will walk in Your truth; unite my heart to fear Your name" (Psalm 86:11).

This psalm showed me that I could always ask God to show me the way to walk in truth. All I had to do was be sure that my heart was bowed before Him in loving fear of His great character and wonderful name. When I submit my will to His will, I choose to fear and reverence Him and seek His ways for my life. I can look at life from a more global point of view, from God's eternal perspective, rather than being distracted by the difficulties and vanities of life. I learn to see my life more through His eyes than from my own limited perspective. I learn to "walk by faith, not by sight" (2 Corinthians 5:7).

Something I've come to understand and treasure through these years has been that God, as a good Father to me, is more concerned with my character and spiritual well-being than He is with me having an easy life or always getting what I think I need. Hebrews 12:5-6 says: "My son, do not regard lightly the discipline of the LORD, nor faint when you are disciplined by Him; for those whom the Lord loves He disciplines, and He scourges every son whom He receives."

In verse 10 of that same chapter it says, "[God] disciplines us for our good, *so that we may share in His holiness*" (emphasis added). Holiness means perfection. It means beauty, goodness, and constantly flowing love. How wonderful that God Himself is responsible to build real holiness in my heart if I will just submit to His ways and His will. His ultimate goal in my life, as a loving and good Father, is to build in me the character and heart of Christ, which is pure love and goodness.

And yet, to my comfort, God understands the struggles and the pain these times of trial and trust can bring. Hebrews 12:11 affirms what we feel about hard times: "All discipline for the moment seems not to be joyful, but sorrowful; yet to those who have been trained by it, afterwards it yields the peaceful fruit of righteousness."

God understands the tension in our hearts as we wrestle with ourselves to make mature decisions of faith. He knows the sorrow we face battling against sin in a fallen world. He understands that we bristle in the depths of our souls against the seeming injustices of life even as we seek to cultivate faithfulness in our lives.

Though it often seems that we end up weary and with dismally few tangible results for all our hard work at faith, we still find God's peace in the midst of it. Because we were made to live by faith and made to be righteous, when we submit to the training of God's loving hand, we end up with peace, a true peace that transcends our circumstances:

> Be anxious for nothing, but in everything by prayer and supplication with thanksgiving let your requests be made known to God. And the peace of God, which surpasses all comprehension, will guard your hearts and your minds in Christ Jesus. (Philippians 4:6-7)

When we submit to God, only then do we begin to sense that we are a part of divine destiny as we bring God's righteousness to bear in this world through our own lives. When we believe truth, we receive truth.

As I look back on that winter in Vienna, I am a bit amused at my own naïveté at that point of my journey as a young mom. Why, the battle was just beginning! Little did I know that I was in for many more such times of faith-stretching struggle. And of finding God's faithfulness.

ㅤㅤㅤㅤㅤㅤㅤㅤㅤ☙

The next years would bring constant battles for my children—for healthy bodies, productive lives, and spiritual depth. There would be years ahead of numerous asthma attacks, ear infections, and respiratory problems. We would move fifteen more times, struggling in each new place through lonely months of adjustment. There would be seasons of financial stress, struggles in marriage, conflicts in churches, and criticism from family and friends for our high ideals with our children.

Two miscarriages would grieve me deeply. Even with my sweet children, the realities of childhood—immaturity, sibling rivalries, and all the rest—would keep me learning and trusting. Not to mention that they would all want to eat every day and wear clean clothes.

The desire for time alone (such as my hour in the coffee shop) would become a recurring theme of longing in my life as my children's needs grew bigger as they grew older. I was mystified trying to find solutions to learning disorders, physical and mental problems with a couple of my children, and behavioral issues in their lives at various stages.

Yes, the good times had just begun when I had that hour alone as a young mother. Over the years, even knowing what I had learned from that time, I can remember times when the burdens of life felt excruciating, when I felt hopeless and abandoned. Yet that planted flag still stood—I would choose to keep walking in faith through the darkness, believing in God's goodness and faithfulness, and waiting for Him to answer my prayers. The consequence of living by faith at such times has indeed, in ways mysterious to me, produced in me the character of Christ. His training (the concept itself infers a long period of exercising discipline) has indeed made me more patient in life, more aware of God's goodness in the world around me, and more willing to love others as He loves me. And I have finally discovered that the universe really doesn't revolve around me.

Many years of difficulties have helped me to become so much more adequate and equipped for ministry. I have a deep compassion for others who are struggling because I understand their struggles from personal experience. I have learned that I have never been in control of my circumstances or my children's hearts, but God is always there and completely able to handle any complexity or trouble that comes my way. I am more humble, knowing my own sin and weakness, and I find my heart being more thankful each day for His patience, forbearance, and forgiveness of all my sin and failures.

I am more content with and appreciative of the internal things—His will and ways in my life, His love, the love and respect of my children, the beauty of life and His creation. By not getting all the things I wanted, and thought I needed, I have found that those things would not have satisfied the deeper longings of my soul after all. Yet I can see that often, as in my young motherhood times, God has to pry my hands open, lovingly but firmly, to help me release the chaff of my will, desires, and petty needs that I so long to hold on to.

When I submit to God's discipline, I find His love to be more than enough, and the thing or circumstance or relationship I felt I needed ceases to be as important. I have learned to live more freely, knowing that God is good and that His way in my life actually provides more joy, freedom, and peace in the end.

As sinful and mortal human beings, we are so attached to this world and its temporal pleasures. Even as believers, we are deeply entrenched in worldly ways of thinking and living. Unless God lovingly loosens our grip on the things of the world, we will never be as likely to long for Him, and we will never learn to desire eternity in heaven with Him, where our lives will finally be free from the burdens of this world. Part of the reality of struggle and the need to trust God in it is the reality that we are being fitted and prepared for a heavenly kingdom of un-spoiled beauty, perfect love, and eternal pleasures and purposes. We are also being freed, day by day, from the things that keep us temporally tethered to this present world, so we can "set [our] minds on the things above, not on the things that are on earth" (Colossians 3:2).

All of this comes through a committed resolve to walk in truth. The key to experiencing these priceless eternal treasures is actively choosing to walk in truth. We live by what Scripture tells us to be true. We read the Bible and set the stories and promises of God before the eyes of our hearts (see Ephesians 1:18) so we can be devoted and loyal to our Father. Only then are we able to believe the truth about His character and walk it out in our lives.

ೞ

Even if you have decided to walk in truth, you must always be aware that the world will entreat you with its deceptions. The voices of this world will try to distract you from God's truth. "Fulfill your own desires. Seek your own pleasure," the world says. "Why are you denying yourself the natural desires and needs of your mind and body?" I have had Christian friends try to give me permission to do whatever I could to escape difficulties and times of stress, and it was a battle to recognize their well-intended advice for the unintended deception it really was. The world tells us that if we are having a hard time, we must immediately get relief. If marriage is hard, get a divorce. If a job is difficult, quit and find another one. If a child creates stress or has problems, let someone else take care of them. If a friend betrays you, break your commitment to that person and find another friend.

However, when we forfeit the ways of God in our lives for the path that offers the easiest way out of pain or stress, we lose the opportunity to grow in maturity, strength, insight, wisdom, compassion, and love—the only things that can ever make anyone really happy. God designed us to possess all these qualities, but if I choose to give up when times get hard, I will forfeit all of God's intended treasures for me, and even forfeit friendship and companionship with the Lord of Life. But if I choose to walk in truth, I walk with the source of all beauty, comfort, and strength beside me. As I submit to His will as His child, and observe how He relates to me as a heavenly parent, I learn a pattern for becoming a good parent to my own children.

Contrary to the world, Scripture tells us that if times are tough, we must keep going—persevere, endure, cultivate patience. This message is strong in the book of Hebrews, written to a community of Christians who had developed a strong testimony and had exercised great faith in God. Yet these faithful believers had been worn down by difficulty and fear of persecution. They were tempted to abandon their faith and return to the security of Judaism. The writer calls his readers to endure in their faith and to not turn back. In Hebrews 10:35-36 he tells them (and us): "Therefore, do not throw away your confidence, which has a great reward. For you have need of endurance, so that when you have done the will of God, you may receive what was promised."

God's will for me and for all His children is not to meet all our needs, solve all our problems, or make our lives easier. He does not want demanding, spoiled children. He has something much more valuable in mind for us. He teaches us to be content, at rest, and strengthened by joy right in the very middle of our very muddled lives. He offers real joy, real strength, real blessing in the world. Those real treasures, gained by submitting my will to God's, are the real life of Christ I can give to my children. God's gifts to me become my gifts to them.

For my children, just as it is for me, living in a fallen world will mean their lives will be hemmed by difficulty, stress, disappointment, and sadness. However, as I learn to find joy amid my difficulties, my children have a pattern to follow. They become familiar with the right ways to respond to God in the midst of trials by having seen it lived out in their own home, in my life.

Without discipline, we can create a demanding child who is often miserable and out of control from not getting his or her own way. However, children who are lovingly instructed and guided will find themselves at peace as they learn, even at an early age, to accept the limitations of life. Children who are trained by loving restraint, and who learn how to find fun and life within those restraints, are more content with less.

Consequently, as we learn to walk in truth by submitting our wills to believe in God's goodness, and to wait on His timing and provision in our lives, we learn how to be good parents ourselves. God provides us a pattern through our own walk with Him of how to walk with our children. They too will grow up to be men and women who will accept His will in faith, and end up with a full share of His holiness. They will lead faithful and fruitful lives that display the character of Christ.

☙

But back to the café in Austria.

After draining my last sip of mélange (cappuccino) with the same savor with which I finished my quiet time, I sat up straight in my chair and resolved to seek to really walk in the truth of my Lord. I would be a loyal daughter to my heavenly Father. I would choose to believe in His goodness and to wait on His solutions. I would walk in His truth.

By the time I got home, after actually enjoying my twilight walk through the shadowy snow, my heart was lighter. Nothing had changed on the outside, but I had grown in my trust in Him and had journeyed quite a way in my soul as a result. Somehow, I actually felt full of joy to be in my snug little Austrian home. I reveled in the wet kisses of my wiggly toddlers and knew that I would simply continue on one step, one day at a time.

This heart attitude has taken me long miles on my journey in life. As I look back now, I can say with David in Psalm 37:25, "I have been young and now I am old, yet I have not see the righteous forsaken." Through the ups and downs of life, God has shown me a pattern of walking with Him and setting His truth before me that would strengthen me and give me peace for many seasons to come.

Pray with Faith

DEAR LORD ❧ Sometimes You seem very far away. When I look at the circumstances of my life and all the prayers that have seemingly gone unanswered, I am tempted to doubt Your love and commitment to me. Sometimes I feel my labor is in vain. I feel lost and alone. ❧ But your Word tells me You are always near, and that you will never leave me or forsake me, and that you are my Helper (Hebrews 13:5-6). Speak to my heart through Your Holy Spirit and through Your Word. Help me to stand firm in my belief in Your loving-kindness, even in the midst of battles both in my life and in my heart. ❧ You are "my strength and my shield" (Psalm 28:7). Help me to resist Satan's desire to cause me to listen to the doubts that swirl about in my heart. Strengthen my resolve to stand on Your wonderful character through every trial and temptation, and keep me faithful to You every day until I see You face to face. ❧ You have stretched me in my life over the years to help me conform to the image of Christ. I want to stand on the foundations of truth each day, each minute of my life's journey. Keep me from stumbling. Help me to walk faithfully with confidence because you are walking with me. ❧ I come to You in the truth and power of Jesus' name. Amen.

☙

Walk by Faith

"Teach me Your way, O LORD; I will walk in Your truth; unite my heart to fear Your name" (Psalm 86:11). According to this verse, how do we learn God's ways? What does it mean to "fear" His name?

"For Your lovingkindness is before my eyes, and I have walked in Your truth" (Psalm 26:3). Are you walking in God's truth? What does that mean? Does God's truth lead you to discover his love and mercy, or does God's truth become a burden of rule keeping for you?

If we as parents are spiritual warriors in the battle for the souls of our children, what kind of "boot camp" experience do we need to be trained for battle? What must we learn in order to help our children learn how to fight their own battles? Hebrews 12:11 says, "All discipline for the moment seems not to be joyful, but sorrowful; yet to those who have been trained by it, afterwards it yields the peaceful fruit of righteousness." According to this verse, how will we sometimes feel in the midst of the battle? If we keep our eyes on the ultimate outcome, which is the fruit of righteousness in our own lives, how can that truth give us the incentive to endure?

CHAPTER ELEVEN

Letting God's Love Fan the Flames of Motivation

Above all, keep fervent in your love for one
another, because love covers a multitude of
sins.

1 PETER 4:8

Another holiday season had come and gone in what seemed like a winter blizzard of endless activities, memories, good food, and laughter. It had been a busy December for the Clarkson family this year, filled with a multitude of greatly anticipated out of town guests, Christmas teas, cookie swaps, crazy kids, and teenager parties. We had, of course, too many hot chocolate and cookie breaks, but they were a perfect accompaniment to our traditional round of family movies and late nights, which left us lots of time to talk, laugh, and eat. Of course, we'd also had far too little sleep.

With all the wrapping of presents, cooking of feasts, and decking of halls, the house was deluged with more than its normal amount of catch up: dirty clothes and sheets, piles of mail, and empty cupboards in my kitchen. All good mothers know that the holiday season puts a huge extra load on mom's shoulders, but we hope that somehow the reward of having our children cherish their memories of home and family will be worth it all in the end. It had certainly better be.

That's not to say, though, that toward the end of December I don't begin to yearn for getting back to our regular routines. Regular life does, at times, seem so much more manageable. The first Monday of this January found me thankful to be past the craziness. Finally, we could get back to some sort of rhythm in our day-to-day lives. I got up feeling ready to whip everything back into shape, but as I began listing what I needed to do just to subdue my domain, and then started walking through the house, I began to feel rather overwhelmed.

Adding to the taming and cleanup from the holidays, I had an upcoming book deadline looming over my head. A busy traveling and speaking schedule, and helping my older children to finish college applications, further threatened my inner peace and replaced it with a feeling of panic as I walked from room to room.

In every room something caught my eye that reminded me of another thing I needed to do, especially regarding my children. Joel's college application sat unfinished on the couch. Nathan's shoes lay in a pile by the door. There were messes for which someone needed reprimanding, issues of diligence to be addressed, and someone needed to feel responsible for the piles all around. And then there was schoolwork and lessons to be planned and arranged. And the list seemed to go on. Real life began to feel as complex and overwhelming as holiday life, but not nearly as much fun.

"I can't possibly do it all! I can't get it all done. It's too much for one person," my feelings kept whining. I found myself mentally making lists of things to be done and framing the right words to communicate those tasks to everyone else who lived in my house. They would need to get going and "get with it" in order to whip our home back into shape.

Hurrying through the breakfast dishes, I barked orders to the late-waking boys about getting back to our family chores and routines as they left for classes and work. It was the first day back to the grind and I was intent on having everyone back up to speed post haste. On my way to put in my third load of laundry that morning, I straightened a stack of books I had selected to read to Joy and grabbed her math book as I passed by, determined to have a good first day back at homeschool.

"Go ahead and start trying to work on these problems," I told her as she crept sleepily down the stairs. "I'll be with you in a moment." I was just getting my mom-work engine revving to get things done.

When the soap had been measured into the washer, I grabbed a pile of clean shirts and ran upstairs in a huff to Sarah's bedroom to find out when she was leaving for work and why it took so incredibly long for her to remember to get her laundry off the dryer. I knocked on her door loudly, still catching my breath. Her muffled voice from the other side of the door calmly bade me enter. I pushed the door open in a great hurry, feeling a need to keep up my momentum. As I stumbled in, though, the sight of her stopped me dead in my tracks. I just stood there and, for an instant, was quiet.

Amid my own hurry and bustle to get the day started, any thought of a moment of personal quietude was forgotten. Surely with the holidays we'd had enough times to sit still and enjoy beauty, but apparently Sarah didn't think so. She was beginning her January in quite a different way, and I was magnetically drawn into her world. She sat in her maroon chair, regarding me quite serenely with a book in one hand and a pen in the other. Haunting piano music greeted my ears (the soundtrack to the new *Pride and Prejudice* movie), and three tiny vanilla candles flickering in different spots around the room greeted my eyes.

The unhurried beauty of the room was strongly present all around me, evidence of Sarah's determination to make room for loveliness and serenity in her days. She had matted small prints and postcards from our trips and arranged them along her walls and in lines above the shelves that held her numerous and much-beloved books. A barely wilting Christmas rose stood in a tiny crystal vase on her windowsill, and there were pine branches still green and fragrant in a woven basket by the door.

A basket of cards along with some lovely stationery and her favorite writing pen sat next to her roll top desk, guarded by the brightly painted eyes of her nested, wooden Matryoshka dolls from Russia. I noticed a new picture on her shelf, a brightly sketched pair of birds by an artist she had just discovered in Canada. There was color, symmetry, and music everywhere I looked. I was confronted with the richness of a soul made visible in the world it created, and quite determined to enjoy this moment despite the rush of life. I felt stopped in my tracks by the sudden presence of this choice to begin the busy day in a moment of soul-enriching beauty instead of my frenzied worry and hurry. I felt I was somehow catching my mental and spiritual breath.

"Hi, Mom," Sarah said sweetly, raising her eyebrows in a can-I-help-you sort of look. I waited a minute before replying, giving my stress-revved pulse time to decelerate. "Here's your laundry," I said slowly when my breath came back. Still absorbing the peace and tranquility of her room, I didn't even remind her that it had been sitting on the dryer for two weeks. Nor did I make note of the lumpy pile of new laundry, expertly concealed with a blanket next to her closet. I simply smiled and took the paper she handed me as I walked out of the room.

I had thought the note she handed me was some sort of information or To Do list, but as I glanced down I saw that it was a card for me, written just that morning. Dropping into my desk chair, I opened it slowly and began to read:

Sweet Mom,

Just thought I'd tell you I'm praying for you as you go back to routine life. I just know that God is going to bless you soon. You are so faithful and have such an enduring heart (I've been reading Revelation and one of the big themes I've caught is endurance), and God is going to bring greatness and beauty out of your perseverance. God will redeem all of us kids because of you. He'll bless you with the fulfillment of your dreams, and He will make my way and all of our ways straight before us. He will do something new!

So don't be discouraged as you sit and pound away at your book and tame all the messes. Great things are going to happen and I love you so much—and that's got to count for something.

So blessings and love and peace of Christ be with you.
Your Sarah

In that moment I felt as if I had been given a special gift through my gifted daughter. It was as if in the rush of my day, God had put it on her heart to stop me in my tracks and call me back to a spirit of calm and beauty. Sarah embodied for me what my soul held so dear—a life reflecting the beautiful reality, goodness, and love of God because of her filled soul.

Sitting in my chair and catching my breath, I realized that in my sudden rush of feeling overwhelmed, I had completely lost sight of what mattered. Yes, the house needed to be cleaned, and presents delivered to their various new owners' spots, and food needed to be bought for the cupboard. But it was all so our home would be a haven, a place rich with life and warm with thought, love, and beauty. My spirit that morning, though, was one of frenzied worry that cared only that things get done, not that people be loved or life enjoyed.

Glancing up as I thought this, my eyes caught a glimpse of Sarah's present to me that year. For Christmas she had given me a hand-drawn scene of an old country home by a pinewood, bathed in the light of a brightly setting sun. In the sunset sky, she had inscribed one of my favorite verses for the year in carefully formed calligraphy:

The LORD is the portion of my inheritance and my cup. You support my lot. The lines have fallen to me in pleasant places; Indeed, my heritage is beautiful to me. (Psalm 16:5-6)

Beautiful to me. Sarah represented a physical reality of the philosophy that the Lord wants me to continue to embrace. The Lord's presence in my life is beautiful, and I want my spirit to be one that accepts it in thanks and appreciation—even on post-holidays, every January, Monday mornings. I thought of how Sarah had recently told me on one of our walks that the things she most remembered and the times that most shaped her were from our long times together: the reading times, the walks, the long discussions, the "girls only" nights out.

"All the things that I have picked up over the years are there because you loved me and chose to spend huge amounts of rich time with me. To me, that is the most precious gift."

Hmm, she didn't say a word about how glad she was that I had trained her to be responsible and neat. She did have those qualities (most of the time), but it seemed that her heart was engaged because I had loved her and taken many long hours to shape her life. Her soul and room and words were an expression of who God had made her to be, but also in part a reflection of the time I had spent pouring into her life and giving her love, beauty, and calm instead of impatience and hurry. Now, I took this all into my own soul, letting my spirit stop running.

Instead of hurrying downstairs, I took a deep breath and walked away slowly, planning what I would do next. I consciously made a decision to brush away my previous mental list of important things to accomplish and replaced it with the high priority of focusing my efforts on how to communicate love in the hours left in my day.

I put on the kettle to make Joy a cup of vanilla-almond tea. I lit every candle I could find in my little living room and turned on my favorite Celtic music CD. I lit up the gas fireplace so that we could have a glowing fire, and made a piece of buttery cinnamon toast to accompany my little girl's tea. Then I called her in and invited her to snuggle up next to me on our cozy, overstuffed couch. I kissed her sweet head and told her how glad I was to have time alone with her. We finished reading *Heidi* together, cloaked in our own spell of beauty and intimacy.

The house was quiet as everyone had left, and in that sweet moment with Joy, the messes and "musts" faded in the face of this sweet little girl and the hour of beauty with which I was forming her soul. I knew that this was what really mattered.

At the end of our time and to my great surprise, she suddenly turned her eyes to me very tenderly and said, "You know, Mom, I would rather have time alone with you than all my Christmas presents and parties. I missed you when we were so busy. I just love it when we spend time alone. It makes me feel so special."

God had used Sarah to gently remind me that, after all, I had another sweet girl just waiting for me to help her become another princess for His glory. And it wouldn't require hurry or bustle or irritation at the busyness of our lives. It required love, and love expressed tangibly through time, words, and lots of beauty. Love, it seemed, truly is the greatest after all.

ଔ

Our lives as mothers are often filled with hurry driven by chores, lists, and a multitude of responsibilities all clamoring "Do it now!" in our spirits. There are so many ideals we feel we absolutely must live up to:

clean houses, ordered lives, and children who accurately know math and Scripture and play their instruments perfectly, besides having just the right amount of friends and activities. We spend hours, days, and weeks rushing about to get all of these things accomplished, trying to keep the house in somewhat perfect order and the people within it in rhythm with all the demands such activities impose on us. In the face of so much urgent need, our "Martha" minds often overpower our "Mary" hearts as we contemplate how to get it all done.

Yet these insistent demands and ideals, the constant busyness and bustle, are not what will actually reach the hearts of our children and shape them into beautiful souls. My focus as a mother is not just on making my children behave, but on helping them become.

Christ did not create disciples who, because of their love for Him, would be willing to die for Him simply because He gave them an impersonal list of moral rules or commandments on how to live life. He did not run training sessions on ministry and servant leadership. He did not have lessons or planned activities to teach them how to live in love.

What He gave them was the gift of His own very present life. In the gospel of Mark it says he chose the twelve so that "they would be with Him" (3:14). They experienced His love intimately throughout the moments of their days. He showed them what it meant to be both a servant and a leader as He invested His days by healing, comforting, and compassionately sharing His loving redemption with needy and humble people. His disciples learned to love children because they saw Jesus letting them climb in His lap—He spoke to them, treated them with dignity, and acknowledged their childlike but real faith. They learned to love each other because Jesus loved them every minute of their days together for three years.

Our model for how to create loving souls is Christ. Jesus showed us as mothers how to disciple our children by modeling it for us with His own disciples. He laid down His life, not just in death, but also daily with the souls He was shaping. This is what mothers do as well, laying down our lives for our children in order to create disciples for Christ with deep, rich souls. Jesus asks us to love our children in the same way that He loved His own disciples.

Paul said that to live in this way was to "walk in love" (Ephesians 5:2). When he charged the believers in the book of Ephesians to walk in love, he pointed them to the model of Christ Himself (verse 1). Paul told them (and us) to love "just as Christ also loved you and gave Himself up for us, an offering and a sacrifice to God as a fragrant aroma" (verse 2).

Paul says that walking in love in such a manner is a fragrant aroma to God—it brings Him glory and pleasure when we walk in the way He walked on earth, and the way He desires for us to walk as well.

If I could only encourage mothers to follow one principle of wisdom in their relationship with their children, it would be that of cultivating fervent, intimate love with each of their children. When children feel loved and cherished by the parents who brought them into the world, they have enduring stability and a security that provides them with groundwork for understanding the God of the universe who so loves us. Love is the most important foundation for learning to believe in God. It is the foundation stone of true friendship, marriage, and parenting. Love, expressed and lived out in relationship, communicates respect and honor to others. As our children are honored with our time, words, caresses, and nurture, life is deposited in their souls. They learn love not only as a personal value, but even more as a tangible experience.

It is interesting to me to observe the high priority that Peter, Paul, and John place on love in all of their writings. These men were eyewitnesses to the life of Christ (or in Paul's case, a vision of Christ) and experienced Him personally from their relationship to Him.

I especially appreciate Peter's emphasis on love because Peter was the one famous for denying Christ on the night of His crucifixion. Earlier, Jesus had told Peter that he was the rock upon whom He would build His church, and yet Peter publicly abandoned Him. How did Jesus treat Peter? With condemnation and criticism and disappointment? No. Only with love and encouragement. He told Peter that Satan had requested to sift him like wheat but that He was already praying for him that his faith would not fail, and that after he had turned back to God he would strengthen the brethren. Peter knew what unconditional *agape* love looked like because Jesus' love for him didn't change even when Peter turned his back on God.

Thus, Peter's charge for us to "fervently love one another from the heart" (1 Peter 1:22) is given within his affirmation of all that God's fervent love has done for us to redeem us and give us new life (see 17-25). Out of that truth, he admonishes us, "Above all, keep fervent in your love for one another, because love covers a multitude of sins" (4:8). Fervent love is intentional and intense. It seeks out, it forgives, it makes new. In the same way, we are to love and express love to our children intentionally, generously, and fervently.

Of those three grand biblical writers, the apostle Paul wrote with an especially deep understanding of Christ's unconditional *agape* love for us. Paul actively persecuted Christians and did his utmost to crush the early communities of believers. But Jesus Himself confronted Paul on the road to Damascus, and in that confrontation Paul must have found a love that reached deeper than any he had ever known. After his conversion, the rest of Paul's writings undergird the importance of love. First Corinthians 13 is his magnum opus of defining unconditional love. Where did Paul learn such love? By knowing the love of God in his own life. Love, he tells us, is the greatest gift. Love will abide forever.

❧

As we walk this path of motherhood, our children will find innumerable ways to challenge our authority, offend our values, and thwart our best efforts to disciple and nurture them. It's the nature of growing from immaturity to maturity. Yet when we walk in love, freely giving our lives to our children, they are able to see our hearts and wholeheartedly respond to us and the God who makes us who we are. In showing them God in our own lives, we need always to keep in mind Paul's words of affirmation that "the kindness of God leads you to repentance" (Romans 2:4).

We walk in love by pouring our sympathy on their small hurts, our encouragement on their accomplishments, our comfort into their trials, and our unfailing belief into the unique ways God has designed their personalities and abilities for His glory. Every day, every minute, we should allow love to determine our attitudes, words, and actions toward our children.

Determining to "walk in love" with our children also frees us from the fear that someday they may fail in life. But here's the reality: They will fail, no matter how perfect we are, because they are human. And we will fail, too, because we are fallen. But God does not ask us to be in perfect control of our children and their lives. He asks us only to emulate His love, which we see modeled in Christ's love for His own disciples. This love held fast through their desertion of Christ right through into their redemption and the sacrifice of their lives for His glory. It was love that held them, strengthened them, redeemed them from their sin, and gave them the will to believe Jesus would work miracles through them. Christ's love never let them go.

Jesus said, "By this all men will know that you are my disciples, if you have love for one another" (John 13:35). But they will also know it by our love for our husbands, for our friends, and by our tenacious, deep love for our children as we walk through the years of motherhood with them.

So today, know that there just might be a precious little one waiting on your couch, in your yard, or in some corner of your home who has a deep need to know the love that both you and God have for him or her. God designed His love to be expressed to your children through your hands, your words, your face, your voice, your service, and your time.

When you walk in love, you become God's channel of love and validation of the great worth of your child's soul. Your love validates and nurtures your child in a way that no one else on earth can. Your love fills up their spiritual and emotional cup. To your child, you are literally the hands of Christ, the love of God touching them.

God truly is, first and last, beginning and end ... love.

Praying with Faith

DEAR LOVING FATHER ≈ *Thank You that You are a God of relationship—that any moment day or night, You are there to respond lovingly to my prayers and my needs. Through Your Spirit and Your Word I know the love You have for me, and for my children.* ≈ *Help me, in the midst of the tasks of life—dirty dishes, bills, messes—to take time to enjoy my children and to delight in loving them. Help me to see deeply into their hearts, to remember that they long for my love, friendship, and commitment most of all. Teach me to fill their cups emotionally, spiritually, and physically so they will have the resources they need every day to meet the challenges and temptations they will encounter. Give my children the ability to receive and know the love I long to give them.* ≈ *Thank You for modeling to me, through the patient, gentle, and generous love of Jesus toward His disciples what it looks like for me to be that picture of love in my own home. Thank You for listening to me and loving me as Your own child.* ≈ *In Jesus' name, because of His life and love, I come to You. Amen.*

☙

Walking by Faith

In what ways do you "walk in love" and communicate love to your children? Is there a specific way you can change your schedule in order to better invest intentional love in their lives? What is one loving thing you can do for each of your children this week? (Write a card and leave it under her pillow, invite him to your room for a cup of hot chocolate and a time to talk, play with her or do a craft or cook with him.)

Jesus said, "Greater love has not one that this, that one lay down his life for his friends" (John 15:13). How did Jesus show His love and focused attention to His disciples? What is one word your children would say that characterizes your relationship with them? In what way would the Lord have you grow in tangibly expressing your love for your children?

"Since you have in obedience to the truth purified your souls for a sincere love of the brethren, fervently love one another from the heart" (1 Peter 1:22). Peter was the disciple who turned his back on Jesus during the crucifixion, yet he was restored to leadership by Jesus' gracious love. How does it make his advice in this verse more relevant as an admonition to us as moms? How can we "fervently love" our children "from the heart"?

CHAPTER TWELVE

Walking the Path of Motherhood with Endurance

Therefore, since we have so great a cloud of
witnesses surrounding us, let us also lay aside
every encumbrance and the sin which so
easily entangles us, and let us run with
endurance the race that is set before us,
fixing our eyes on Jesus ...

HEBREWS 12:1-2A

What I've said before, I'll say again—Prince Edward Island is, without a doubt, one of my favorite places on earth.

Known simply by its initials, PEI is a small, windy island on the far eastern edge of Canada, made famous by Lucy Maud Montgomery's *Anne of Green Gables* books from the early 1900s. My girls were raised loving the "Anne" books and movies with their tales of Anne Shirley and her dreamy adventures on her beautiful island. So when we had the chance to visit this fabled place on the tail end of a speaking trip in New Brunswick, we jumped at the chance. None of us knew exactly what to expect, and having dreamed about it for so long, I was slightly afraid that the island would be modernized and ugly, nothing like the quiet farmland and shadowy forests found in the Anne books.

To my utter delight, Prince Edward Island was one of the few places in the world that entirely exceeded our expectations. Driving in, I felt as if my pulse was slowing just at the sight of the beautiful land and brightly colored fields. When we arrived at our inn after a long day of driving, it was like stepping into the rich, well-ordered world of the past, complete with quiet evenings, rocking chairs, and morning walks on a deserted beach. Prince Edward Island had managed somehow to become a world apart. The rush and invasiveness of modern life had never gained a footing there, and the island felt and looked much as it must have when Lucy Maud was imagining and writing her beloved stories there.

The island didn't even get electricity until the 1950s and, in keeping with the wholesome island feeling, billboards seem to have been banned once you get beyond Charlottetown, its capitol and main city. Barely a mile outside of the city, you are already into the countryside on a winding road that loops through miles of pristine farmland. The fields are hemmed by deeply green and very old fir trees that shade tiny old wooden farmhouses with those famous and very darling gables.

There was still a value for the old kinds of beauty on the island, with gardens and lawns kept like works of art, and fields spilling over with wild lupines. Travel not very far in any direction and you will soon reach seashore—blue and windy places of rocky coasts and heaped sand dunes that run down to the cold northern water (but not cold enough to keep my kids out of it). I would rarely see a single other soul on the beach, and our favorite daytime activity was to walk for hours, sand between our toes, collecting the choicest pearl blue oyster shells and smooth white clam shells.

At the inn where we stayed, there was nary a television to be found, and we almost immediately fell into an easy, old-fashioned rhythm of fresh meals at lovely tables together, and hours spent outside in nature's beauty. Most of our time found us simply enjoying God's good creation—in fields with flowers, with books on the porch, on long walks on moonlit beaches, and talking in the gable room with the windows open to the fresh air. Peace and rest seeped in at every corner.

Since that first visit, Prince Edward Island has become a sort of haven for our family. We can't make it up there very often, of course, but when our souls are weary with work and ministry, and we have managed to save our pennies, it is our secret place in which to take a very refreshing refuge. Tucked away from the ravages of the modern world, we get to live just for a little while in a quiet place spilling over with peace and natural beauty. We always come back refreshed.

This thought was in my mind as I sat at my desk and pondered our summer. I was deeply exhausted—more tired than I could remember being in years. I was running on empty. Even beyond my physical exhaustion, I found a soul weariness overtaking my spirit.

We had met recently with some Christian publishers, trying to explain our vision of training mothers to make biblical choices for the sake of their children. Put simply, it was draining. Our strong convictions about choosing a lifestyle that provides time with children to build a relationship and to pass on a legacy of righteousness seemed only to elicit responses such as, "We like what you are doing, but we don't want to print anything that would ever make anyone feel guilty," or "We feel that moms have the right to make their own decisions without the consequence of any unnecessary guilt."

This was surprising in the face of statistics that nearly half of American young adult children do not adopt the values and religious beliefs of their parents. Faced with that disturbing statistic, I was feeling discouraged and wearied by the publishers' lack of response. Sitting at my desk, I began to yearn for the quiet and restoration of a visit to Prince Edward Island. The idea grew into a strong desire, and after thinking about it for a while and taking an account of the summer ahead, I decided to begin exploring the possibility of a trip.

This would be the "girls club" adventure of chapter four. When I asked Clay about it and he was generously agreeable, it felt like divine affirmation. Even though finances were tight, all of us girls could go away to Prince Edward Island together to rest, relax, and be refreshed. The thought of that time coming was like an oasis to me in a desert of weariness. With the trip ahead of me, I managed to make it through the rest of the next month. Finally, after packing the boys off to a music camp and arranging a thousand and one details, we girls got up early on a summer morning and headed for the Denver airport.

Three connecting flights, one very bumpy bus ride, one pleasant jaunt through an overcrowded customs checkpoint, and a day later, we arrived in Charlottetown, Prince Edward Island. We were travel worn and weary, but we had made it. After a long and leisurely dinner that night, we snuggled into our old farmhouse beds and fell fast asleep.

And on the first day, we rested. Like God at the completion of His creation, we simply reveled in the beauty of the world around us. We walked on the beach, soaking in the fresh air and quiet, quite thrilled at the novelty of our newfound freedom from all responsibility and need. The second day dawned cool and cloudy, suggesting the possibility of rain later in the afternoon, but the morning was full of promise.

It was a perfect morning for a long beach walk, but having walked much of the beach the day before and feeling a little adventurous, we began pondering our options for some new walking itineraries. Since we had been at this lovely guest farm two years before, we were somewhat familiar with the area. The last time we were here, we had driven from Shaw's Hotel, where we were staying, to Dalvay by the Sea, the grand old summer mansion that sits on the northern shore. We knew it better as the White Sands Hotel, where many familiar scenes and events in the Anne movies and series were filmed.

In our memory, the hotel wasn't that far up the coastline, and we thought it might be a challenging but still reasonable walk. We didn't have a car that day, and since we wanted adventure, we decided to try it. When we asked about it at the front desk, the hotel owner casually encouraged us, "Well, it is a bit of a walk. I would say about four miles. If you take it slowly, you can make it."

We'd walked four miles together many times before, so that was all we needed. Loaded with a couple bags full of the necessary umbrellas, water, and sweaters, Sarah, Joy, and I donned our favorite walking shoes and took off along the beach highway. It was cool and just overcast enough to shield the sun. We felt confident and together. After walking at a hard pace for forty-five minutes (poor Joy had to stretch her little legs to keep up with us two tall women), we came to a small lighthouse that was the first landmark we were to locate. Since Joy had been fading in spirit for the last few minutes, we decided that a five-minute break was in order.

"Mom," Joy said in her trying-to-be-spunky-but-worn-out voice, "you know that I am usually a trooper, but you are walking too fast today, and I am tireder than I thought I would be and one of my feet is hurting." There was a hint of tears in her brown eyes.

Sure enough, the beach shoes she had worn the day before had rubbed a small blister on her foot that had grown irritated with our last hour. I gently placed a Band-Aid on the sore spot, stroked her long golden hair, and apologized for walking too quickly today.

Joy is a bright little girl, full of vim and quite ready to take things on. Having grown up with two older brothers immediately above her and a sister beyond that, she was full of energy as she kept up with everyone. I told her I thought we were halfway there, and that we could either go back now or press on ahead and have a fun treat at the hotel. As she was sitting beside me on the sandy stone steps of the lighthouse, I could almost see the emotions battling it out in her little head, and I knew it could go either way. Either the weariness and feelings of "I can't go on another step" were going to take over, or she would resolve to make it.

As is often the case with Joy, the determined strength of her heart spread right out of her eyes and onto her face. "Mom, I would hate to quit just because I am a little tired. I know I can make it if I just keep going one step at a time." She even managed a smile.

We began again, taking the road at a slightly slower pace, confident that we could relax a bit since we considered ourselves more than halfway there. The cloud cover had actually given us a nice blanket of cool weather to trudge along in, and though we were warm enough to have shed all the sweaters, we still felt cool enough for comfort. I was admittedly getting a bit warm, though, as my handy tote bag swelled with everyone's discarded clothing and water bottles. But I straightened my shoulders, lifted my chin with a confident smile, and even attempted some cheerful conversation to distract the girls for what I thought would be our last forty-five minutes of walking. It worked and we all grew progressively bright in spirit, bolstered in our confidence that we were nearing the hotel and a lovely teatime

At the end of those minutes, though, I was a bit surprised that Dalvay by the Sea was nowhere in sight. We were just about to reach a national park marker, so I pulled out the very simple map I had from the hotel in hopes of encouraging the girls with how close we were to our destination. I glanced at the map, matched our current location to its little icon on the road, and then blinked. I wanted to clear my eyes to read again what I was sure I had misread. But the page in front of me didn't change. According to this map, we were barely halfway there.

Halfway!? The innkeeper had said four miles, and I knew without a doubt we had walked at least five. Sarah and I are both daily walkers averaging a mile every fifteen minutes, and even with Joy in tow, we had still been walking almost two hours. That hotel should be right around the next bend. I just crossed my fingers and prayed that the map was quite a bit off in distances. Sarah cast me a very pregnant glance after catching a glimpse of Joy's tired and slightly irritated eyes. We dared not even hint to our spunky little girl that she might have to go as far again as she already had come.

"Must be just ahead. See, up there, around that clump of firs way up there."

We turned and started at it again, Joy with her head down. Sarah walked a little ahead hoping to catch a glimpse of the hotel. We were a quiet bunch now, too engrossed in our walking to talk much, no longer pretending to be peppy. Five minutes later the sun tore open our cloud cover and shone its full blazing glory on our faces. I had administered sunscreen, but the blush of heat was soon visible on both the girl's faces as we trudged on, now with our heads down. We were beginning to grow weary, to say the least.

Another half hour passed. The sun continued to blaze down on our reddened faces with no compassion, the wind died down to nothing, and each bend brought yet another familiar line of pines and long grey road, but no hotel. We trudged on. *I remember another walk like this,* I thought, going back in my mind to our day lost in the mountains behind our home in Colorado.

Just as before, I thought of how brightly we had set out on our walk, but bemoaned our bedraggled state now. Sometimes it felt as if everything we attempted was hard. As my legs grew tired, my heart grew weary, too. The road began to narrow now as well, curving in upon itself so that we had only a thin strand of gravel to walk on as cars whizzed by.

We passed some beautiful natural park trails and occasionally glimpsed the toss of the ocean in the distance, but with the sun out and our energy low, we had few resources left with which to enjoy any of the scenery. Besides, we walked mostly on pavement through high sandy hills that obstructed our view of the ocean and of what was ahead. Since I was afraid of finding us even farther behind, I didn't really want to check the map against the signs we passed.

After another thirty minutes I felt that surely we would find the hotel. I had glanced at the map enough to know there was one big curve that would signal our approach to it. Often, we would be walking toward a curve in the road that looked like the curve on our map, but curve after curve brought no sign of the longed-for hotel, and time and again our hope was disappointed.

I glanced at my watch. We had been walking for two-and-a-half hours. We were bedraggled and dog-tired, with our heads down, eyebrows furrowed, and sweat dripping down our noses. On a day that was supposed to be fun and restful, we looked pretty pitiful! Joy was openly in tears though still quite determined. I found myself irritated with the universe. I looked up to find yet another curve was just ahead. I rolled my eyes and plodded around it, sure we would be disappointed again.

But there, sitting smugly by the road, was a sign. There was no hotel, but there was a sign that told us we had just two kilometers to go, just over a mile. I looked at the girls and they looked back at me. We gritted our teeth and steeled our spirits for that last mile. With this bit of hope we could make it. Joy's chin came up, and we all took a deep breath and began to walk a little faster. As if to aid us, the clouds managed to overcome the insistent sun and a cool wind breathed lightly around us as we walked.

When the first gable of the old mansion peeked out from above the firs, Joy gave a whoop and managed to run a good ten steps before deciding she would finish our marathon at a reasonable walk. Finally, our feet swished through the thick green lawn of the hotel, and then we climbed the familiar stone steps and entered by the great oak doors. As the doors clicked shut, I just stood there for a moment to catch my breath and slow down my racing thoughts.

We'd made it. Hallelujah!

When we were settled in our seats, flushed and triumphant, we smiled at each other. We guzzled down our fresh, cold water and munched on our rolls as the waiter took our order for tea and the traditional toffee pudding. Just before our tea arrived, the manager came over to chat with us as guests for a moment. Asking where we were from and where we were staying, she listened as we reported that we were from Colorado and were staying at Shaw's Hotel just down the road. We also let her know, just as an aside, that we had just walked from there to Dalvay that morning. At this, the woman's jaw dropped and she literally gasped.

"You are kidding, aren't you? Why, it's almost impossible to imagine that this little girl could make it that far. Do you realize that she walked at least fourteen kilometers, nearly ten miles! You are some kind of hero! Congratulations!" She spoke loudly enough for the nearby tables to hear, and held out a congratulatory hand to Joy.

Exhilaration and profound joy burst over Joy's face as brightly as the sun had that morning. She took the proffered hand and gave it a victorious shake. When the woman had gone, she turned to me with a conspiratorial grin and whispered, "Wow, Mom, can you believe we walked ten miles? I feel so proud that I finished and didn't give up!"

This became our story of the week and made Joy a special hero. Exclamations of surprise and admiration followed wherever we went. We did indeed keep to less strenuous days after that (and we didn't ask opinions on distances from the hotel staff), but that walk became legendary. In the end, it was perhaps the favorite memory of our trip.

Joy still talks about her heroic walk. As grueling as it was, she is immensely proud that she conquered it and made it to the end. Our unexpected adventure has stuck with us ever since—heart, mind, and for me, soul. As I have pondered it, I have come to some rather interesting conclusions about our long walk and its likeness to my life as a mother.

ೞ

The memory of our adventure was still fresh as I spent time with the Lord one morning soon after our return from Prince Edward Island. The physical endurance required by that walk—the way we kept on, kept hoping, kept being disappointed, and yet somehow made it to a glorious end—blended with my prayers over the emotional and spiritual weariness I was feeling. As I pondered it again that morning, I realized that our never-ending walk was an analogy to my life, particularly as a mother.

In the same way that Joy started our walk to Dalvay, I started out on the journey of motherhood with such bright stars in the eyes of my heart. I had assumed it would be a lovely adventure that I would be able to accomplish with vibrancy and grace. I did not have a realistic understanding about how much longer this walk in life with my children and husband would be, or about the blisters, hot sun, rough pavement, and curves I would face in the road ahead.

My dreams before motherhood were full of cuddling my darling babies, rocking them, and nurturing them in our first years together. I was the youngest child and only girl in my family growing up, so I was protected and a bit spoiled. I was rarely around young children, so I was unprepared when I had babies, and did not comprehend just how much longer and more difficult this path of motherhood would become.

I hadn't counted on the weariness of years of being pregnant and nursing, of giving birth and having miscarriages. I didn't have a realistic understanding of the many phases of motherhood that would demand all my strength—asthma, ear infections, tantrums, messes and fusses, thousands of mounds of dirty dishes and clothes, and countless days to fill with meaningful occupation, not to mention the training, correcting, and instruction of my children in righteousness.

I had no idea how often loneliness would literally overwhelm me as I strove to learn and become all that I needed to be for my family without the help of mentors or support systems in my life as we moved so many times. I had no comprehension of what homeschooling my children would cost, or the effort that four children of different needs, personalities, and disabilities would require.

Yet many times, when I was tempted to quit taking so much time from my own life to give to my kids, and when I felt like I simply couldn't go on, I would creep away into my quiet corner to spend even a few minutes with the Lord. Without fail, He would use those stolen moments to show me how important my role was in the spiritual life and heritage of my children. In those times, I glimpsed the goal of righteousness I was working toward and realized that I must "put my head down" and reach it step-by-weary-step. Those times gave me the resolve to take one more tiny step.

The single resolve to keep going one step at a time kept me moving forward. It wasn't by feelings that I continued on, for life was certainly never easy, nor was it because anyone else agreed with me. Most of the time I struggled through long conversations with my family and people at church who felt my life at home with my children was unnecessary and extreme. It wasn't even because I had a crystal clear understanding or promise of what was ahead. Rather, I kept going by faith and resolve because I could not ignore the ideals and calls of Scripture.

With God's help, I have always chosen to follow the ideals He has put in my heart, to trust that they are right and will bring blessing to me and my family. Just as we did on our endless walk on Prince Edward Island, I put my head down and keep on walking, trusting that God's goodness is ahead. I choose, by the grace of God, to walk this road every day, and to keep on seeking the ideals I see so clearly in Scripture.

☙

So we come to the end of this book. Whether you are standing just on the cusp of motherhood or you have already journeyed a long way as a mother, you can make today a new beginning, a new commitment to walking the path of motherhood with God with your whole heart. There are so many more things I could say, and I could write still more books just to encourage you as you walk the path of motherhood. But I'll just say a few more words to close this book.

Over and over in Scripture, we are reminded that these children of ours are made in the image of God, and their souls will last for eternity. As a mother, you are the first shaper of a soul that will last forever. Mothers were designed by God to be the champions for their children's souls. God did not entrust children to the church, to neighbors, to groups, or to schools, but to parents.

It is my conviction that God designed a mother to be the essential life-giver in her home domain. We are the heart shapers, the formers of eternal souls and spirits. We are the heart of our homes. Our homes, our love, our will to give life and celebration, to portray grace and goodness—these will be the factors that shape our children into adults who will love God and His kingdom, and who will change the world.

Don't ever give up. Stay on the path. Keep on walking.

On that long walk on the Prince Edward Island beach, we would have shortchanged our great victory if we had quit at any point. To have someone say, "Oh well, I guess it was just too far to walk," would never satisfy like hearing, "Well done! You made it all the way." I want to know I took the long road of motherhood and to hear God say, "Well done!"

During that week on Prince Edward Island I read a book about the days of Jeremiah (*Run with the Horses* by Eugene Peterson). I was struck with how similar our days are to those of Jeremiah's. He preached God's ideals for twenty-three years to a people who ignored him, mistreated him, and despised him and the message he brought from God. He was tempted to throw in the towel and quit.

But God reminded Jeremiah that he was not responsible for changing the hearts of the people. His role, his holy work, was simply and faithfully to hold up the ideals that God had built into his heart. He was to show God's purpose through a life of integrity and wholehearted commitment to the Lord lived out faithfully even in the face of rejection.

As I think about Jeremiah's life viewed through the lens of our own long walk on the island, it was as though the Lord reignited a flame in my heart. I heard His whispers in my soul, filling my mind and rising to a chorus in my heart:

> *Keep walking. Keep reaching for God's ideals. Keep following Me. Your work as a mother after My heart does matter. Your desire to please Me and faithfully complete the journey I have set before you will have eternal significance. So keep walking. Stay on the path, and don't give up. Keep walking. I am with you every step of the way. Keep walking with Me.*

That is my last word to you, my friend. May God encourage you to be a finisher of your mom walk, a faithful soul in your long journey of motherhood with Him. May your heart be strong in love and faith toward your children, always seeking to see God's hand and work in their lives. May your heart be strengthened to endure, in marriage and parenting, through storms and troubles. May you determine to walk *your* path of motherhood, the one God has placed *you* on, with His eternal purpose, assurance, trust, and heart.

May your love for our sweet Lord stay ever strong and may His love sustain you through every decision, every day, every difficulty, and every joy. May you find in Him the strength to choose well and to persevere in your choice. May your soul be filled and your spirit overflow with celebration and joy as you journey through life as a mother with your Savior. May you feel the grace of God beneath your feet with each new step of faith along God's way of life. You are blessed and beloved.

Walk well the path of motherhood.

Praying with Faith

DEAR FATHER AND CREATOR OF LIFE ❧ *You have designed my role as a mother to teach my children to love You and walk with You. I also understand that this journey of motherhood is long, and that Your path for my life as a mother may not always be easy.* ❧ *Help me, Lord, to learn how to walk according to Your plan. Help me to have strength and wisdom for each season, each day, each footstep of my journey through life with my children. Give my children a heart to respond to You and to me as we walk together on this journey.* ❧ *Give me the grace and strength to endure through all of the hardships along life's way with joy and peace in my heart. Help me not to sacrifice my ideals along the way in discouragement, but make me one who finishes strong and well because of Your power and grace working through me. Give me courage. Help me to persevere so that I will one day see the fruit of my loving labor in heaven, and rejoice. Make my precious children into those who will follow You their whole lives, and bless the generations of my grandchildren after them.* ❧ *I will follow You, Lord. I will not give up, or be tempted to leave Your way. I will resolve in my heart and spirit to walk my path of motherhood with purpose, assurance, trust, and heart because You are walking with me. I dedicate all of my days of mothering to You.* ❧ *In the name of Jesus, who walks this path with me. Amen.*

☙

Walking by Faith

"[L]et us also lay aside every encumbrance and the sin which so easily entangles us, and let us run with endurance the race that is set before us" (Hebrews 12:1). Is there anything you need to do to simplify your life in order to be able to run without "encumbrance"? Is there anything you need to "lay aside" that might trip you up as you journey through motherhood? Are there any secret sins in your life that "entangle" your spirit and "encumber" your walk with Christ. Name them (write it or them down here), confess any sin to God (1 John 1:9), accept His forgiveness and help, and then keep running your race.

Hebrews 12:2 tells us that the key to endurance in this life is "fixing our eyes on Jesus, the author and perfecter of faith, who for the joy set before Him endured the cross, despising the shame, and has sat down at the right hand of the throne of God." How does fixing your eyes on Jesus help you have faith and keep going amid the difficulties of your walk today? If you believe that there will be a reward at the end of your own race—that your labor of faith, love, prayer, and patience for your children will make a difference—how does that influence the way you walk with God now?

What are the most important things you have learned from this book? Is there anything you can put into practice right now to more faithfully walk your PATH of motherhood with purpose, assurance, trust, and heart? What can you do, starting today, to make sure that you will complete your walk of motherhood—your mom walk—to God's glory?

My Mom Walk
with God

PATH
Journal

I Will Walk with PURPOSE as a Mother

Older women likewise are to be reverent in their behavior, not malicious gossips nor enslaved to much wine, teaching what is good, so that they may encourage the young women to love their husbands, to love their children, to be sensible, pure, workers at home, kind, being subject to their own husbands, so that the word of God will not be dishonored.

Titus 2:3-5

_____

_____

_____

_____

_____

_____

_____

_____

_____

_____

_____

_____

_____

_____

PATH Journal: PURPOSE

I Will Walk with ASSURANCE as a Mother

For by grace you have been saved through faith; and that not of yourselves, it is the gift of God; not as a result of works, so that no one may boast. For we are His workmanship, created in Christ Jesus for good works, which God prepared beforehand so that we would walk in them.

Ephesians 2:8-10

_____

_____

_____

_____

_____

_____

_____

_____

_____

_____

_____

_____

_____

_____

PATH Journal: ASSURANCE

I Will Walk with **TRUST** as a Mother

Trust in the LORD and do good; dwell in the land and cultivate faithfulness. Delight yourself in the LORD; and He will give you the desires of your heart. Commit your way to the LORD, trust also in Him, and He will do it. He will bring forth your righteousness as the light and your judgment as the noonday.

Psalm 37:3-6

PATH Journal: TRUST

I Will Walk with **HEART** as a Mother

Therefore if you have been raised up with Christ, keep seeking the things above, where Christ is, seated at the right hand of God. Set your mind on the things above, not on the things that are on earth. For you have died and your life is hidden with Christ in God. When Christ, who is our life, is revealed, then you also will be revealed with Him in glory.

Colossians 3:1-4

PATH Journal: HEART

_____

_____

_____

_____

_____

_____

_____

_____

_____

_____

_____

_____

_____

_____

_____

_____

_____

_____

_____

_____

_____

_____

_____

Trust in the LORD with all your heart
and do not lean on
your own understanding.
In all your ways acknowledge Him,
and He will make
your paths straight.

— Proverbs 3:5-6 —

But the path of the righteous
is like the light of dawn,
that shines brighter and brighter
until the full day.

— Proverbs 4:18 —

About the Author

Sally Clarkson is the mother of four wholehearted children—Sarah (1984), Joel (1986), Nathan (1989), and Joy (1995). She is a popular conference speaker and the author of numerous books and articles on Christian motherhood and parenting, including *The Lifegiving Home* (with Sarah Clarkson), *Own Your Life*, *Desperate* (with Sarah Mae), *You Are Loved* (with Angela Perritt), *The Mission of Motherhood*, *The Ministry of Motherhood*, *10 Gifts of Wisdom*, and *Seasons of a Mother's Heart*. She is an active blogger on SallyClarkson.com, and a regular podcaster on "At Home with Sally."

Sally joined the staff of Campus Crusade for Christ (now Cru) in 1975 upon graduation from college. After working briefly with students at the University of Texas, she moved overseas to minister to women in Communist Poland and throughout Eastern Europe, and then returned to Colorado in 1980 to minister to single adults and executive women. Since her marriage to Clay in 1981, she has continued to minister to women and mothers through personal discipleship, small groups, speaking and teaching, and conferences.

In 1994, Sally and Clay started Whole Heart Ministries to encourage and equip Christian parents to raise wholehearted Christian children. Sally has written books and articles, published a newsletter for mothers, spoken to Christian and homeschooling parents in workshops and conventions, developed and trained leaders for the Mom Heart Ministry initiative, and built an active online ministry. Since 1998, Sally has ministered to thousands of mothers through her WholeHearted Mother and Mom Heart Conferences. She has spoken internationally on four continents and her books have been translated into Chinese, French, Dutch, Korean, Spanish, and other languages.

Sally loves the companionship of her family, thoughtful books, beautiful music, holiday traditions, classic British drama, strong English tea, walking, traveling, and eating out (so someone else does the dishes). The Clarkson family home is in Monument, Colorado in the foothills of the Rocky Mountains and the shadow of Pikes Peak.

About Whole Heart Ministries

Whole Heart Ministries is a 501(c)(3) nonprofit Christian home and parenting ministry founded by Clay and Sally Clarkson in 1994. Its mission is to encourage and equip Christian parents to raise wholehearted Christian children. Strategic ministry initiatives include motherhood, spiritual parenting, Christian home, home education, and books and reading, For more information contact:

Whole Heart Ministries
P.O. Box 3445 | Monument, CO 80132
719-488-4466 | 888-488-4466
whm@wholeheart.org | www.wholeheart.org

Keeping Faith in the Family

About Mom Heart Ministry

Mom Heart Ministry is a strategic ministry initiative of Whole Heart Ministries birthed in 2010. Its mission is to restore moms' hearts to God's heart for motherhood by cultivating a movement of small groups for mothers. MomHeart.com provides training and resources, and the Mom Heart Groups Facebook group provides an online community for moms who lead groups and minister to other moms. For more information about Mom Heart Ministry, contact Whole Heart Ministries (above), or visit the MomHeart.com website.